FROM TURNER'S STUDIO

David Blayney Brown

From Turner's Studio

PAINTINGS AND OIL SKETCHES FROM THE

TURNER BEQUEST

TATE GALLERY

'From Turner's Studio'
a Tate Gallery Collection exhibition
is sponsored by Digital Equipment Company Limited

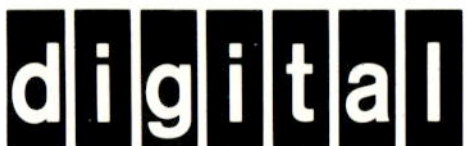

cover
Shipping at the Mouth of the Thames *c.*1806–7
detail (cat.no.7)

ISBN 1 85437 062 6

Published by order of the Trustees 1991
for the exhibition touring to
Bristol Museum and Art Gallery: 15 March – 5 May 1991
Walker Art Gallery, Liverpool: 17 May – 7 July 1991
Glasgow Art Gallery and Museum: 19 July – 1 September 1991
Aberdeen Art Gallery: 21 September – 9 November 1991
Sunderland Museum and Art Gallery: 23 November 1991 – 19 January 1992
Ferens Art Gallery, Hull: 1 February – 22 March 1992
Derby Art Gallery: 4 April – 24 May 1992
Castle Museum, Norwich: 6 June – 26 July 1992

Reprinted 1992
Designed and published by Tate Gallery Publications,
Millbank, London SW1P 4RG
Photography: Tate Gallery Photographic Department

Typeset in Monophoto Sabon by August Filmsetting, Haydock, St Helens
Printed and bound in Great Britain by Balding + Mansell plc, Wisbech,
Cambridgeshire on 150 gsm Parilux Cream Matt

The Digital logo is a trademark of Digital Equipment Company Limited

CONTENTS

SPONSOR'S FOREWORD

The works in this catalogue, spanning almost half a century, give a thorough appreciation of the development of a great artist.

This is the first time that these paintings have travelled in the United Kingdom since the Turner Bequest has been housed at the Clore Gallery beside the Tate Gallery in London. I am particularly pleased that we at Digital have been able to help introduce them to a wider audience.

We specifically wanted to support an initiative which allows more people across the country to gain access to the nation's cultural heritage. After all, it is by making information available wherever it is needed, regardless of geographic boundaries, that we have grown to be the world's leading supplier of networked computer systems.

Digital is no stranger to the arts. Our 'Partners in Arts' programme, begun in 1986, embraces dance, theatre and music. Most recently, we sponsored the record-breaking 'Monet in the 90s' exhibition at the Royal Academy.

This latest venture will, I am sure, bring a great deal of pleasure to art-lovers across the country. We are delighted to be associated with it.

Geoff Shingles CBE MANAGING DIRECTOR
Digital Equipment Company Limited

FOREWORD

Since the death of J.M.W. Turner in 1851, his Bequest to the nation has undergone many vicissitudes. His paintings and drawings were for a long time divided between the National Gallery, the Tate Gallery and the Print Room of the British Museum. Only in 1987 were almost all of them united in the Clore Gallery, adjoining the Tate Gallery beside the Thames at Millbank. Following their installation in their new home, it seemed wise to leave the pictures undisturbed for a period, so that the collection might be seen in its entirety and in order to allow fragile paintings – and indeed their frames – a spell of rest and stabilisation. However, it has also been our wish to share them with a wider audience, and it gives us special pleasure that the first significant group of paintings to leave the Clore Gallery since its opening should do so to tour a group of galleries in the United Kingdom.

Turner's intentions for the whole collection of pictures remaining on his hands had not been made precise in his various wills. They were still undefined at the time of his death, for it seems clear that by then it was only the 'finished' pictures, numbering about a hundred, that he envisaged hanging in the 'Turner's Gallery' which he wanted to be built at the National Gallery. However, later generations have had cause to be grateful to his family, who by their machinations to overturn his will ensured – though unintentionally – that the nation received all his work, both finished and unfinished.

Today we value the insights into Turner's mind and methods to be gained from his unfinished pictures, sketches and studies as highly as the complete statements he exhibited and sold. In this spirit, the pictures for this exhibition have mainly been chosen from that body of his most personal and intimate work which he would never have put on public display in his lifetime, but in which his powerful imagination and inquiring intelligence are to be seen operating as intensely and vigorously as anywhere in his work.

Many colleagues, both at Millbank and in the regions, have been involved in the preparations for this exhibition. May I thank them and also the Directors of the museums and galleries where the exhibition will be shown. The Tate Gallery values their hospitality. We look forward to further collaborations with the major museums and collections across the country, as we endeavour to fulfil one of our most important aims, that of sharing the national collection with regional audiences.

Finally, we are delighted that Digital Equipment Company Limited has agreed to sponsor the complete tour of this exhibition. This is a great encouragement to all the eight venues and we offer them our sincere thanks.

Nicholas Serota DIRECTOR
Tate Gallery, London

The unity that the human spirit gives to vision can only
be found in the studio. It is there that our impressions,
previously scattered, are co-ordinated and enhance each
others' value to give the true poem.

Camille Pissarro

INTRODUCTION

When Turner died in 1851, the gallery of his house in Queen Anne Street West contained a lifetime's accumulation of paintings. The spectacle was both magnificent and melancholy. Once a splendid room with deep red walls and excellent lighting, the gallery was now dilapidated, and the pictures hanging or stacked around it were in decay. Turner had hoarded them but not looked after them. 'What does it matter?' he had apparently asked a visitor who remarked on a large lump of paint that had fallen from one of the noblest pictures in the room, 'Crossing the Brook': 'The only use of the thing is to recall the impression'. Another picture, 'Fishing upon the Blythe-Sand', now beautifully restored (cat.no.9), seems to have been in commission as a cat flap.

Yet these, and other works in adjoining rooms, were the pictures Turner had intended for the nation. There were others besides, still more neglected, whose future the artist had failed to elucidate. His wishes changed somewhat in the course of the wills, and codicils to wills, that he made between 1829 and 1849, and although his aim in 1832 had been 'to keep my pictures together', it is by no means clear whether he referred to absolutely everything remaining in his hands, or to 'pictures' in the understanding of his own time. Certainly his final wish was for his 'finished pictures' to go to the National Gallery, and to hang in rotation in an additional 'Turner's Gallery'. It was when his family, who had received nothing, overturned his will in order to obtain such money as was left in the estate, that the gallery received everything adjudged to be from his hand 'without distinction of finished or unfinished'.

It was an extraordinary assemblage. There were pictures among the most important he ever painted, but had never sold; others he had bought back, doubtless with an eye to posterity, or had received from their purchasers in exchange for other works. The rest were the survivors of his studio – oil sketches and studies, some still on long rolls of canvas; pictures begun but not completed; canvases laid in but never pursued; and a number of those dazzling variations on themes elemental or atmospheric, peculiar to Turner himself, to which conventional demarcations between finished and unfinished seem superfluous to the modern eye.

It must have been these last that impressed Elizabeth Rigby, a visitor to the gallery during Turner's last years, as 'matchless creatures, fresh and dewy, like pearls just set – the mere colours grateful to the eye without reference to the subjects'. Miss Rigby's opinion was characteristically advanced. The first displays of the Bequest at Marlborough House in 1856, organised in part by her husband, Sir Charles Eastlake, followed Turner's own wishes in displaying very largely the finished works, while the others remained in store at the National Gallery, unaccessioned and unappreciated. Canvases like the late sunrises (cat. nos.26,27), or even more daring abstractions of colour and light in which the paint appears to take on a life of its own and to play on the painter's imagination rather than to describe its fancies, had to wait until the advent of Impressionism for curators and critics to reconsider them with the benefit of hindsight. Since their first exhibition after 1900, they have occupied a special place, even among the more idiosyncratic works in the

Bequest. But it would be a pity if they were to obscure the many other private faces of the artist, or to dominate our ideas of his objectives throughout a long working life.

The richness of the Bequest is in its variety. Besides finished pictures, it contains not only the inspired effusions of his final mastery, but the essays and experiments of his youth, and, from the years between, a multitude of sketches in which we may trace the development of his imagination and technique. It is mainly from these more personal works that this exhibition has been chosen. Here is not the 'public' Turner, the painter of show-stopping exhibition pictures for the Royal Academy and the British Institution – and even for his own gallery. We should imagine Turner at work in the privacy of his studio, testing compositions and effects, colour and tone, seeking solutions and solving problems, and at times literally playing with paint; sometimes, also, we must picture him sketching from nature in the fields or from a boat, or improvising away from home in hotels or the houses of friends.

Whether or not this was Turner's intention, it is for these insights that the Bequest is so precious a legacy. There is no lack of descriptions of Turner at work, but they are usually rather dramatised, and based on his deliberately theatrical performances for the benefit of his colleagues on Academy Varnishing Days. But what of the canvases he brought to the exhibition room for finishing? What of the sketches and studies he made without regard for his audience, in order to learn, experiment or clarify his ideas? How a great painter sets about the making of his art; how he develops his technique and imagery; how he decides what is important to him, and what is not – all are questions of compelling interest. But Turner had kept his deepest ponderings strictly private, and left ambiguous, if not

actually false, trails about his practice. It was no accident that his 'Daddy' had for many years prepared his canvases and that his housekeeper, Hannah Danby, had set his palette. To others, as the son of his friend Mr Trimmer recalled, his studio 'during his lifetime, had been enshrined in mystery, and the object of profound speculation. What would his brother artists have given some thirty years before to have forced an entrance when Turner was at the height of his powers?'

Turner himself had been haunted by just such yearnings. In a lecture of 1811 he had spoken of Claude, whom of all the old masters he revered longest and deepest: 'where', he asked, 'through all these comprehensive qualities and powers can we find a clue towards his mode of practice? As beauty is not beauty until defin'd, or science science till reveal'd we must consider how he could have obtained such powers'. He was referring specifically to Claude's evident devotion to study from nature, but such speculations are common to all who gaze on genius, and were rife in Turner's time. In his youth the academic air had buzzed with debate on the methods of the masters, ranging from the empirical analyses attempted by painters like Reynolds or Benjamin West, to the fraudulent reconstructions of Thomas Provis, who claimed to have discovered the secrets of the Venetian masters. But there was no substitute for hard evidence, and so it was that when Turner's studio was opened after his death, visitors fell upon palettes and brushes, boxes and phials, as hungrily as upon the pictures themselves.

But of course it was in the pictures, and not in the dusty clutter of a cupboard, that his genius resided; the mere materials, eccentric or commonplace, were lifeless in themselves. However ambivalent Turner's attitude to the whole content of his studio, he would have been the first to admit its objective value. 'What is the use of them but together?' he once asked, and the question must have been sharpened by the recollection of how he himself had learned his trade. In a time when the practical mechanics of painting were hardly taught at the Academy, these, like the vocabulary of style, had to be learned from the study of other painters; copying, trial and error, were all part of a learning process conducted to a remarkable extent upon the student's own initiative. It was as well, if only opportunity existed, to study pictures in all states of completion, not just finished works. The masters or mentors of Turner's youth had recognised this, and provided their pupils with evidence of their processes and preparations; Reynolds lent pictures 'purposely left unfinished' for copying, and Richard Wilson had left canvases simply 'laid in' to his pupils. Turner's legacy, intentionally or not, offers similar lessons. More than this, it opens his mind to us. Just as he saw himself as the last of the old masters, so his Bequest provides for us just those 'clues' he could only imagine for Claude, Rembrandt or Titian.

✳   ✳   ✳

Of Turner's very first ventures in oil, there is scanty evidence in the Bequest, but it is almost all we have. Turner kept one of his first exhibited paintings, the moonlit 'Study at Millbank' that he sent to the Academy in 1797, and it already proclaims his effective mastery of a style of painting he had learned from the French painter P.J. de Loutherbourg, from whom he had been taking technical advice – a sleek Continental style, that disciplined the paint rather than allowed it a vitality of its own. This was not to be Turner's way for long. Indeed, the abundance of sketches and studies in the Bequest can be read partly as evidence of his lifelong quest for that inner vitality. Meanwhile, the limitations – or rather the inappropriateness – of this surface elegance soon became apparent to a painter who was already moved by the vitality of nature.

While there is nothing to document Turner's assimilation of his 'de Loutherbourg' manner, for no very early oils survived in the studio in an unfinished state, there is plentiful evidence of his rejection of it. A group of small pictures, both finished and sketched, from the later 1790s shows him evolving a technique more characteristically English, more palpably made out of paint. Continental painters tended to use fine-ground colours, laid in near-transparent glazes, and their canvases were prepared generally with pale grounds, related in tone to the intended effect of the picture. English practice was different; painters used darker grounds which were more thoroughly obscured by their denser paint. Their already robust manner was in the 1790s tending to become rougher and more broken under the impact of the prevailing fashion for the 'Picturesque', with its emphasis on all that was rugged and accidental in nature – for the marks the painter made became the very equivalents of the haphazard manifestations of the natural world. The apogee of this taste in Turner's earlier work may be found in the 'Bank with Gypsies' that he probably exhibited in 1809 (cat.no.10), for it is a textbook compendium of 'Picturesque' landscape features, and was shown to the public as a 'Sketch'. While modern debates about 'finished' and 'unfinished' have focused on Turner's late works, it was in fact mainly during his early career that contemporary aesthetics justified the making of pictures of an apparently spontaneous kind, and encouraged their exhibition. Arbiters of the 'Picturesque' like Richard Payne Knight even claimed to prefer sketches to highly finished pictures. In the whole context of Turner's work, and of his attitudes to art, this was a fashionable aberration, but long after the fashion was dead and gone, and its particular mannerisms abandoned, Turner continued to explore the equivalence between the movement of paint and the dynamics of nature. He retained besides his admiration for those old and recent masters he had first studied when constructing his bolder style in the 1790s – Rembrandt, Salvator Rosa and Richard Wilson.

Turner was not, in a complete sense, an original artist. He responded to the influence and challenge of other painters, past and present. The old masters were a constant inspiration. It was through Wilson, only recently dead, that he first learned to love another painter's work. Turner was bound to look up to him as a master of landscape, the field he had chosen for himself. He admired Wilson's subtly atmospheric evocations of Italy and paraphrases of the classical landscape of Claude, but even more, he admired Wilson's introspective side; his spontaneous, unaffected and less deliberately composed appreciation of real scenery in his native Wales or around London. The handling of these other Wilsons is broader than his grander subjects, but his paint is always rich and juicy, his colouring sober and masculine; he was truly a painter's painter, and for Turner, committed to landscape painting, he was a beacon. The Bequest preserves a quite distinctive group of small finished or sketchy pictures from the later 1790s, in which Turner may be seen coming to terms with Wilson's style and handling, and Wilson remained a powerful influence into the next decade if, as seems likely, the mountainous landscape with a castle (cat.no.5) dates from after Turner's trip to the Alps in 1802.

It was natural enough that Wilson, Welsh by birth and the painter of many splendid Welsh views, should spring to Turner's mind when he began to explore North Wales in the late 1790s. Oils like the 'View of a Town' (cat.no.1), very possibly a Welsh subject, reveal him trying out not only a Wilsonian composition constructed along horizontal planes regressing from a dark foreground, but also Wilson's creamy paint and dabs of impasto. Besides Wilson's treatment of pure landscape, Turner was impressed by his historical compositions, the most ambitious union of landscape and the 'Grand Style' yet attempted by a painter in the British Isles, and an obvious point of reference for a young artist whose ambitions were tending in the same direction. A Wilsonian handling, a suggestion – not yet fully resolved – of a tragic subject of death or parting, and the impact of the Welsh mountains combine in the smaller and less developed 'Dark Landscape' of about 1798 (cat.no.2). Here, Turner is perhaps playing with ideas of the 'Sublime' rather than consciously planning a particular picture.

Although still predominant, Wilson was no longer the only influence here. The deep contrasts of light and shade suggest awareness of Rembrandt, and the flickering handling reminds one of Venetian painting; it was at just this time that Provis's 'Venetian Secret' was tantalising the artistic community. Turner was very sceptical of the 'Secret', but he certainly hankered after Venetian tone, and the unfinished state of this little canvas enables us to see that it was painted on a ground of deep salmon pink, no doubt so that this could contribute warmth and depth to the whole. As we have seen, the potential of the ground to modify the finished effect had been well understood by de Loutherbourg. The thick opaque paint and deep tones Turner first used while imitating Wilson's handling led him briefly away from such considerations, but he turned back to them again when soon afterwards he began to lighten his palette and to strive after the cool atmospheric gradations of Claude.

Thenceforward, he almost always used pale grounds. By the time his studio was properly established in the early years of the new century, his father was preparing canvases for him with off-white or pale beige grounds made to his own recipes. Meanwhile, it is instructive to compare early Wilsonian essays in a sombre tonality with a sketch of an historic landscape composition, made about 1800 (cat.no.4). Yet again Wilson is the compositional source, but the colouring is altogether clearer and brighter, and the paint is laid on thinly and transparently, with great animation, over an almost white preparation. Turner was by now taking what served him best from English and Continental practice – the bold, strong touch of the one, and the subtly filtered tones of the other.

＊　　　＊　　　＊

Opposites constantly competed and combined in Turner's imagination and in his art – none more powerfully and creatively than the apparently conflicting claims of nature and art. But Turner was very early aware of opposing attractions in art itself. From Wilson he graduated to two old masters who could not be more disparate; Rembrandt and Claude, whose 'negative quality of shade and colour, that aerial perspective enwrapt in gloom' and 'golden orient of amber coloured ether' he contrasted in a lecture in 1811. The Rembrandt passage alluded to a painting Turner must have seen on a visit to his early patron Sir Richard Colt Hoare at Stourhead in 1795. Claude likewise hung in the house, and it was Colt Hoare who prompted Turner to essay his first finished classical landscape, 'Aeneas and the Sibyl, Lake Avernus' (cat.no.3), in about 1798. Its sober touch and cool colour are still based on Wilson's interpretation of Claude rather than on the master himself,

but it was a first step in a direction that was to produce some of Turner's greatest pictures.

In 1815, Colt Hoare commissioned another view of Lake Avernus from Turner, and both painter and patron may have accepted that the earlier canvas was painted for practice only. It is wholly a studio composition, owing nothing to the painter's own observation – unless of other pictures. Yet Turner's exhibited paintings and their increasingly elaborate titles were by the later 1790s already alluding to particular natural effects or times of day. He was beginning to locate his work within personal experience, and to emphasise the study of nature he was now pursuing so avidly in his sketchbooks. He saw no inconsistency between his studies of art and nature. The 'continual studies of parts of nature' without which he considered Claude's mastery inexplicable, was integral to Turner's art. But it was not self-justifying; as he believed Claude's to have been, it was pursued for what it could contribute to the wider purpose of imaginative composition.

Turner put his case in a famous passage added to the margins of the text of the lectures given by his fellow painter, John Opie:

He that has that ruling enthusiasm which
accompanies abilities cannot look superficially.
Every glance is a glance for study: contemplating
and defining qualities and causes, effects and
incidents, and develops by practice the possibility of
obtaining what appears mysterious upon principle.
Every look at nature is a refinement upon art: each
tree and blade of grass or flower is not to [the artist]
the individual tree grass or flower, but what is in
relation to the whole: admiring nature by the power
and practicability of his Art and judging of his Art
by the perceptions drawn from Nature.

The 'practice' and 'refinement', the search for 'practicability', were constant processes, advanced by thought and experiment and fostered by memory, rather than by sudden impulse. It is clear that work in the studio played at least as great a part as direct observation; Constable was to compare the art of seeing nature to a scientific experiment, but while Turner would have understood what he meant, his own purpose was wider. It should come as no surprise that he was so sceptical of the advantages to be had from sketching in oil out-of-doors – central as this often was to the Romantic perception of nature. He certainly did paint outdoors at various times, but the practice was never of fundamental importance to him, as it was for Constable and later for the Impressionists. It conferred no special legitimacy on the finished product, and certainly did not promote random and accidental effects to the exclusion of other pictorial values.

Turner was less of an outdoor painter, both in oil and watercolour, than might be supposed; and less so than ever during his later years when the economy and spontaneity of so many of his colour studies might suggest an immediate response to the motif. Rapid notations in pencil, and a superbly cultivated memory, were the true starting points of his mature art, as many reliable anecdotes confirm, while his several campaigns of oil sketching from nature produced results of rather limited use to him. The first took place at the turn of the century, in Kent when staying with a friend at Knockholt, near Sevenoaks. Strictly speaking, the studies of woodland that he made at Knockholt and Chevening are not in oil but in mixed media including watercolour, and they are made on paper over pencil under-drawing. A few are brilliantly coloured, but most have a rather unsatisfactory, experimental feel; though they represent as direct a confrontation with pure landscape as can yet be found

in Turner's work, they show little of the freshness of tone that might be expected, and incline instead to the fuscous and muddy. It was a problem that did not go away, and much later Turner told a friend that he rarely used oil in the open air because he always 'got his colour too brown'.

If the Knockholt sketches seem to display less lightening of the palette than a studio sketch like cat. no.4, they do show Turner exploiting the pale surface of the paper as he did in his watercolours, leaving much of it exposed to give the highlights. This habit became more marked in the oil sketches and studies that he made along the banks of the Thames and Wey about 1806–7, on wood and canvas prepared with pale grounds. A number of these seem to have been painted from nature; the panels especially have a bold and immediate feeling, and the young Trimmer recalled that Turner 'painted on a large canvas direct from Nature' from a boat he kept at Richmond. One is reminded of Monet on his studio-boat at Argenteuil, and indeed there seems a premonition, in Turner's brilliant, flickering sketches of the Thames, of the marvellous sketches Monet and Manet made during their stays by the Seine.

Certainly Turner was now assimilating a greater naturalism into his painting of English scenery, and the ready access to pastorol subjects provided by his acquisition of a second home at Isleworth by May 1805, and then of another at Upper Mall, Hammersmith, may well have inspired him to try at least to lay the foundations of finished pictures out-of-doors. The panels are clearly sketches and no more, a controlled – and brilliantly successful – experiment, but some of the canvases seem more than this; they have been quite carefully developed or substantially altered, and if begun on the spot, they were evidently advanced in the studio. Other sketches on a similar scale of marine or coastal subjects, like the animated estuary view (cat.no.7), seem closely related to this phase of Turner's work, but can hardly have been painted outdoors at all. It must also be observed that a highly disciplined pictorial imagination is at work in all these oils, and that the exhibited pictures of the same date were taking on very old-masterly effects, while in his sketchbooks Turner was transposing Thames scenery into totally Claudean vistas of seaports and antique cities. The Thames sketches cannot be regarded simply as studies from nature made in a spirit of unaffected naturalism; nor are they the work of an innocent eye. They are very powerfully designed, and had at least the potential for development into finished pictures. The future cat door, 'Fishing upon the Blythe-Sand' (cat.no.9), could have begun in such a way, and a contemporary sketch of Margate (cat.no.6) was perhaps destined for completion as a coastal scene like the Bequest's 'St. Mawes', exhibited in 1812.

Turner's division of his Thames sketching between small wood panels and canvas – the latter probably kept on a roll and painted in sections that were laid over a wood frame while he was working – evidently proved a serviceable one. He used both materials again in Italy, in 1828, and ordered two rolls of canvas to the Isle of Wight in 1827 when he planned to sketch the Cowes Regatta in oil (cat.no.14). The large majority of his Italian sketches, and some of the Cowes subjects, were to be composition rather than nature studies, and outdoor painting in oil remained an occasional phenomenon in Turner's work. Meanwhile, however, he had tried it again in Devon in the summer of 1813 – a summer of long golden days and a bumper harvest. Induced by his artist friend Ambrose Johns to take his paints into the fields, and provided with a 'portable painting box', he set to work with what observers took to be increasing confidence; some sketches (such as cat.no.11) were apparently made in 'less than half an hour'. Turner was less obviously concerned with re-ordering scenery for compositional effect than in the Thames or later Italian sketches, and indeed his display of some of his Devon views to local friends during a picnic, 'in order to verify them', might suggest a wholly unbiased approach. But appearances can be deceptive and there are in cat.no.11 some significant modifications of the topographic truth. Whatever their real purpose, Turner later dismissed the Devon sketches as 'worthless'. As earlier in Kent, he had worked on paper, prepared on one side with oil, and probably because of some defect in this preparation, the colour relationships were spoiled. More time in the studio, or a more level working light, might have spared him such problems.

The experience can only have confirmed his cautious and ambivalent attitudes to sketching in colour from nature. More than ever, as he thought of his subjects in terms of colour, he thought in the studio – or whatever passed for it when he was travelling. The many hundreds of radiant colour studies or 'beginnings' in which he designed tonal structure in watercolour, and the rather smaller number of such studies in oil, were not made before the motif; they depended at least as much upon a collection of memories as upon specific moments. Nor did colour study play a vital part in gathering essential local information. Thus when he first visited Italy in 1819, pencil memoranda vastly outnumbered watercolours, and – though there was a long tradition of oil sketching from nature going back to Claude, and now refreshed by whole communities of young artists in both Rome and Naples – he seems to have forsaken oil altogether.

No less significant is Turner's attitude to painting when he returned to Italy in 1828. He was now certainly ready to paint, to produce finished pictures for exhibition in Rome itself, and to use oil as a vehicle for exploring and resolving ideas or compositions. Painting outdoors, however, was not part of his plan. As before, beside the Thames, he painted some small panels, and one or two of these do seem to speak of the open air. But of the sixteen studies he painted – thickly and flatly, with occasional dabs of impasto – on a roll of coarse canvas, almost all are pure compositional designs, evocative rather than descriptive; only two can be connected with actual places. They address problems of classic and Claudean arrangement in terms of colour masses, and provided Turner with a repertoire of designs through which to approach the Mediterranean landscape. Beautiful as they are in their abstract way, they were purely functional.

*   *   *

For Turner, Rome, the Campagna and southern Italy were inseparable from the conventions of classical landscape composition – however vividly expressive his appreciation of natural effects. At the same time, this ancient and hallowed world was a domain over which his imagination played freely, nurtured by his reading of history, mythology and natural science. The subject of the tragic lovers Hero and Leander, who may probably be seen emerging from the empurpled gloom of one of his Italian oil sketches (cat.no.18), was one that haunted him for many years, and his very last exhibited pictures were, beneath their diaphanous and spangled veils of paint, entirely Claudean compositions telling the story of Dido and Aeneas (cat.no.29). A play of reference and allusion – the heritage of an artist brought up in a tradition that set academic or historical painting on a pinnacle – remained fundamental to his creative process. Studio sketches and experiments were a forum for exploring these ideas – ideas which sometimes present

themselves quite clearly, or seem still to be evolving, struggling painfully from the depths of the subconscious. In Rome in 1828, Turner sketched and painted the neo-classical nude several times, nearly completing at least one picture of a Venus. Here the imagery is conventional enough, whatever his private motivation. But in the very unresolved sketch known as 'Death on a Pale Horse' (cat.no.12), we are on less sure ground. If this episode from the Book of Revelation was indeed the subject, it was common in Romantic painting, but Turner's treatment seems to owe more to his inner state than to contemporary precedent. And what are we to make of the phantom fleet or column of soldiers that advances through the mists and exhalations of a late sketch usually considered a Venetian scene (cat.no.28)?

If Turner was thinking in paint, we need not expect him to reach firm conclusions. Naturally enough, such inconclusive experiments occur in large numbers from periods of his life when he was setting himself new fields to conquer: historic landscape in the 1790s; pastoral scenery in the first decade of the new century; and, in the 1830s, historical genre. Turner was by then sufficiently affected by popular trends in painting and literature to experiment with romantic or sentimental narrative and period costume pieces. But such subjects did not come naturally to him, and the various sketches of historical figures in sombre interiors, usually associated with his stays at Petworth in the late 1820s and early 1830s, are best regarded as exercises in such compositions to which specific subjects had not yet been attached. In so far as Petworth, where Turner set up a studio in the Old Library, was a source and inspiration for some of these, he was bringing a variety of its suggestions – grand, shadowy rooms lit by shafts of light from great windows or blazing lamps; gatherings of people; the old masters that hung on the walls – to the purpose in hand. To these

[16]

ingredients he added another; a resurgent concern for the chiaroscuro and painterly textures of Rembrandt. 'Dinner in a Great Room' (cat.no.21) is one of these still vague exercises in historical genre and Rembrandtesque effect. It is painted on a canvas of a size Turner used for exhibition pictures, and could perhaps have been brought to completion with the addition of a central incident.

Other oils of the same period are far less resolved. So confused and altered are they, so embryonic Turner's ideas, that there could be no question of working them up into finished pictures. In his later years, Turner certainly recycled old canvases for new pictures, repainting them for exhibition, but the chequered progress of some would have been impossible to disguise. He continued to draw a distinction between canvases laid in and prepared for finish, and others that were for trial, experiment or – lest it be forgotten – pleasure only. Yet the making of such 'separate' sketches did not necessarily imply uncertainty or unfamiliarity with the subject. There is nothing hesitant or unsure about the marvellous oil sketches of Petworth Park and other Sussex subjects painted in the later 1820s, in anticipation of the four pictures he made for the dining room at Petworth. The finished pictures, which remain in the house, are more highly wrought and deeper in tone than their brilliantly evocative predecessors which Turner kept; as in some of Constable's exhibition 'six-footers', an entirely happy inspiration seems somewhat dulled by the restraining hand of Art.

Turner did not usually make full-scale studies for his exhibited or commissioned pictures. Why then did he prepare new versions for Petworth instead of amending the sketches? Was he so fond of the house and its associations that he wanted to keep records for himself, or was he deliberately making sample studies – as he was later to do in watercolour – to indicate to Lord Egremont what was to come, to offer him choices of finish, tone and detail? There is reason to believe that both versions of at least one subject were briefly hung at Petworth at the same time. Possibly, also, Turner needed to acclimatise himself to an unfamiliar format – a wide and low rectangle, dictated by the circumstances of the room; and indeed it seems he may have painted at least one of the sketches *in situ* before continuing work in the Old Library. The unfinished riverscape on the same format (cat.no.13) that has sometimes been connected with a Petworth composition, may also have arisen mainly from his need to experiment with particular effects and spatial arrangements required there.

Turner's sketches specifically for Petworth included a seascape that was not used, and one of the largest canvases in this exhibition (cat.no.16) may also have been begun with Lord Egremont in mind, in Rome in 1828 when Turner was meditating a picture to accompany a Claude at Petworth. With two other large landscape designs, it may have been an alternative composition, prepared before he made his final choice, evidently the 'Palestrina' that, in the event, remained on his hands after exhibition at the Academy in 1830. Left unfinished, these largest of all Turner's Italian sketches joined the growing number of pictures in the studio that could have been completed quite quickly.

*   *   *

As Turner grew older, he saw his studio stock as a reserve on which he could draw. As best he could as conditions deteriorated and untidiness mounted, he would move among his canvases, reconsidering or reworking them here and there, or laying in schematic bones of composition and colour; he still had a stock of canvases, primed by his father, though the old man had died in 1829. 'I believe', wrote G.D. Leslie, the son of painter C.R. Leslie,

> that Turner had for a long time been in the habit of preparing works for future exhibition, laying in, with simple colours, the effect and composition, painting them solidly and very quickly with considerable *impasto*, and allowing the whole to dry and harden together. He would use no fugitive pigments in these preparations... He must, I think, have had many works thus commenced laid by in his studio, from which he would take one, from time to time, to send to the Academy exhibition.

A work like the vividly coloured 'Arch of Constantine' (cat.no.22) was advanced almost to completion in the studio, probably in the mid 1830s. Canvases sent to exhibition would have looked very different. Although they might still, if Turner thought it appropriate, be meticulously painted in accordance with convention, like the historicising 'Van Tromp' seascape (cat.no.20), they gave less and less away on first appearance. In Leslie's words 'like milky ghosts', or as a more hostile colleague, E.V. Rippingille, described, a mere 'dab of several colours, and "without form and void", like chaos before creation', they might have been almost designed to bewilder, in order that the ensuing miracles of creativity should sufficiently amaze. Often 'whacking away with about fifty stupid apes standing around him', as John Scarlett Davis observed him in 1836, Turner would lay scumbles and glazes of clear and brilliant colour over these minimal foundations, working extra-ordinary transformations over the three Varnishing Days. They were not magic – nor as some would have it, madness – but method adapted from his watercolour practice, which had long depended on myriad touches of vivid local colour over a pale surface.

By such infinitely subtle processes Turner gave substance as well as form to his exhibition pictures. They were as densely packed with meaning in the 1830s and 1840s as any he had ever painted; indeed the texture of meaning became more intricate even as form was dissolved in mist, sunshine or wave. This was no paradox, for life, and therefore all the business of art, existed for Turner within the larger drama of the natural world whose springs and motions he now more completely understood, and was bound to register through the marks of his brush. He sought not a limited or specific naturalism, but a wider engagement altogether. His public art was intended to be both particular – as his documentary titles and emphasis upon personal experiences still made clear – and universal. He still tirelessly observed nature at work, and recalled its manifestations in paint – never more powerfully than in his many late sketches, large and small, of seas and beaches and breaking waves (see cat.nos.23–25) – but despite all appearances these entirely private paintings are rarely spontaneous impressions caught on the wing; if they 'recall the impression', it was often at a certain remove, and at the behest of a richly stocked imagination. Clouds and waves, the hint of a ship or a beachcombing figure seem sometimes to emerge almost unbidden from the paint itself, as if some electric charge were leaping between the energy of the painter and that of the elements he was painting. As a young man, Turner had insisted to a surprised Joseph Farington that he 'has no settled approach but drives the colours about till he has expressed the idea in his mind'. He was speaking of his watercolours, but his words would apply still more accurately to his late use of oil.

That one word 'idea' gives the lie to an altogether extempore approach. Moral and emotional perspectives, historical and contempory reference, echoes from the great masters, were ever present for Turner. Their synthesis, their reconciliation with a penetrating understanding of the natural world based on years of looking and remembering, was the daily business of his life, promoted by constant private study and experiment as well as through the work he showed. Hence the absorbing interest of even the humblest contents of his studio. Hence, also, Turner's own deepening awareness of the value of his work 'together' at the end of his life. His last exhibited pictures (see cat.no.29), which he can hardly have hoped to sell, were fantasias on Claude and classical legend filtered through a shimmering, trembling veil of hazy light, while even the most radiantly distilled of the unexhibited pure landscapes of the mid 1840s (cat.nos.26, 27) had been anything but casual or unsystematic. They were lyric poems, as finely judged as anything in his work, exquisitely subtle deconstructions through morning light of the classic compositions and real landscapes he had studied as a young painter. Manet, many years later, would laboriously paint figures outdoors so that they might 'dissolve in the vibrations of the atmosphere'. Turner had achieved this from memory and in the studio, for scenes and subjects drawn mainly from the past.

Turner's mood in old age was often nostalgic, recapitulatory. As he pottered among his pictures, he reviewed his life and art, and his thoughts turned also to the future. The sunrises were in several cases reworkings of subjects he had invented years ago for his codex of landscape, the *Liber Studiorum*, proof that art can renew itself, and that a great painter can transcend his own style. Notwithstanding his own provisions for their future display, perhaps he was beginning to think of the contents of his studio and gallery in their entirety, and wished to leave there some examples of his high pastoral manner, transfigured by his mature understanding; perhaps these were in a sense painted for posterity. But he did not forget his contemporaries. Following the publication of the first volume of Ruskin's *Modern Painters*, with its spirited championship of his art, in 1843, his pictures were again in keen demand, and he was encouraged to put some earlier canvases into repair, and keep by him some finished work, to tempt the new purchasers who now came to the gallery. In 1848 he took the unprecedented step of hiring a young assistant, Francis Sherrell, to help him sort out his pictures. Sherrell preserved a vivid memory of Turner mixing his yellow in a bucket and plastering it on a canvas with his bare hands, but he made little real impression on the house in Queen Anne Street, and after Turner's death there remained much to discover, much to rescue. The task has lasted many years, and is not yet quite completed. Only in this century were some of the less obviously grand pictures restored, or the rolled canvases separated to yield sketches such as cat.nos.6, 7, 14, 17, 18. Turner might be surprised to find that we value them and exhibit them alongside his finished work, but we may be confident that he would understand.

FURTHER READING

A.J. Finberg, *The Life of J.M.W. Turner, R.A.*, 2nd ed., Oxford, 1961

J. Gage, *J.M.W. Turner: 'A Wonderful Range of Mind'*, New Haven and London, 1987

L. Gowing, *Turner: Imagination and Reality*, New York (Museum of Modern Art), 1966

J. Lindsay, *Turner: A Critical Biography*, London, 1966

A. Wilton, *Turner in his Time*, London, 1987

CATALOGUE

Exhibited works are from the Turner Bequest unless otherwise stated. All paintings and works on paper in the Turner Bequest referred to in this catalogue are normally found in the Clore Gallery at the Tate Gallery. Locations are given only for works outside the Bequest and for those few pictures belonging to the Bequest shown at the National Gallery. Measurements are given in millimetres followed by inches in brackets; height before width.

Abbreviations

B & J   Martin Butlin and Evelyn Joll, *The Paintings of J.M.W. Turner*, 2 vols., 1984 (revised edition)

T B   A.J. Finberg, *A Complete Inventory of the Drawings of the Turner Bequest*, 2 vols., 1909

W   A. Wilton, *The Life and Work of J.M.W. Turner*, 1985 (with catalogue of watercolours), (revised edition)

1　**View of a Town**　*c.*1798

Oil on canvas 240 × 325 (9$\frac{1}{2}$ × 12$\frac{3}{4}$)

N 00475

The Welsh landscape painter Richard Wilson was the predominant influence on Turner's early work in oil. Besides his Italian subjects and historic landscapes in the classical tradition of Claude and Poussin, Wilson had excelled in more unassuming studies of pure landscape, treated in subdued colours with a broad handling. Turner's early technique was particularly modelled on this latter aspect of Wilson, and is well displayed here in this small but finished picture. The construction of the composition on horizontal planes with a dark foreground and light-filled sky, and the juicy paint with creamy highlights on the trees and tower on the horizon, are very Wilsonian, while the big rocks in the foreground are features found in a number of Wilson's pictures. The view, though unidentified, is probably in Wales or on the River Wye, for Turner projected his recollections of Wilson's work into his Welsh excursions in the 1790s, particularly the long tour in 1798 during which he visited the painter's birthplace at Penegoes, and which must have been the source of his later reminiscence of 'the days of my youth when I was in search of Richard Wilson's birthplace'.

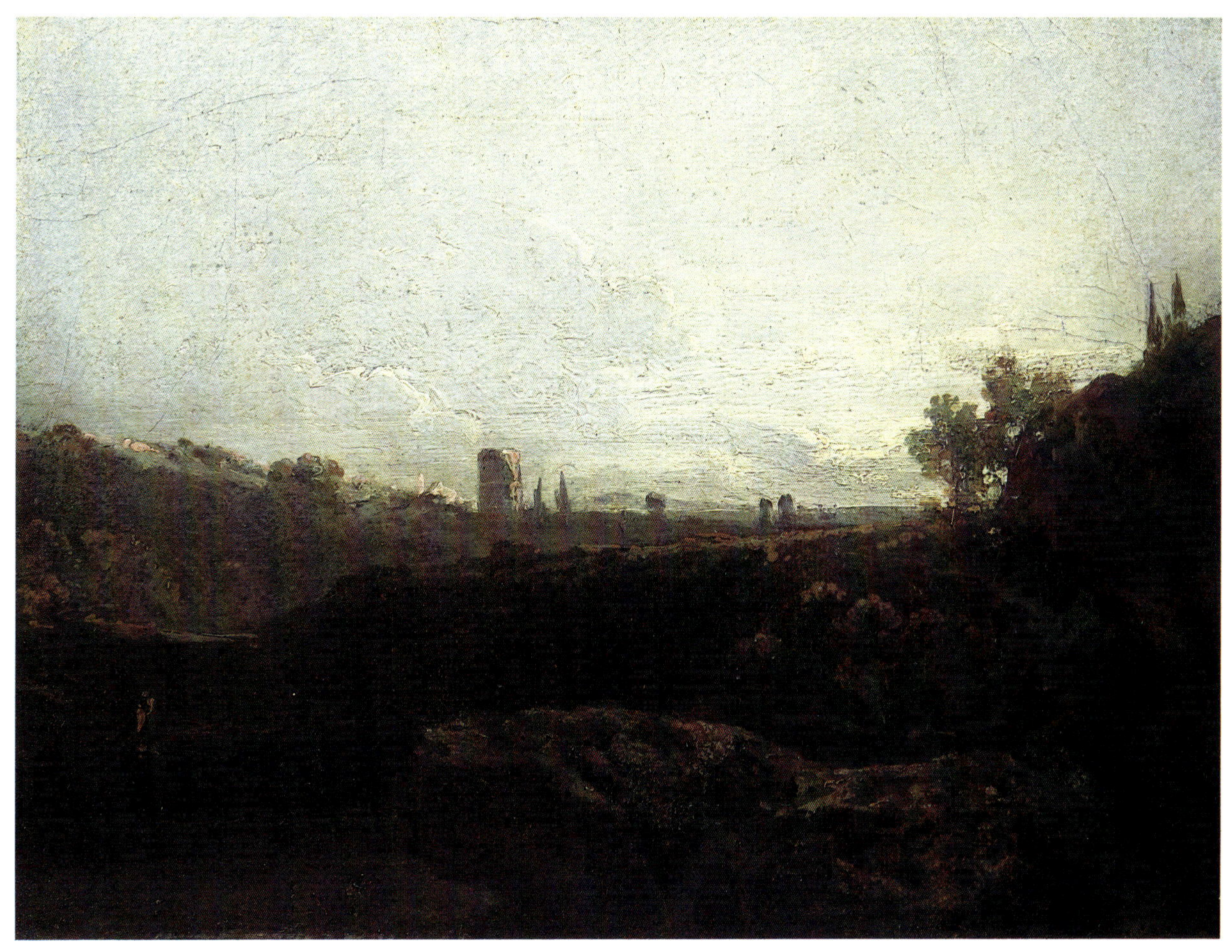

2   **Dark Landscape with Trees and Mountains** *c.*1798–9

Oil on canvas 315 × 390 (12¼ × 15¼)

TB LI M; D 02380

One of a group of spirited oil sketches made in the late 1790s, this bold and sombre work reflects Turner's ambitions towards 'Sublime' historic landscape inspired by Wilson, and earlier masters like Poussin and Salvator Rosa. Turner's training at the Royal Academy, based on the hierarchical standards laid down by its first President, Sir Joshua Reynolds, asserted the moral supremacy of history painting – the 'Grand Style' – and the reconciliation of landscape and epic narrative was a problem that exercised Turner for many years, while those old masters who had achieved it successfully were singled out by him for special admiration and study. Paramount among them was Titian, whose altarpiece of 'St Peter Martyr', now destroyed but to be seen by Turner in the Louvre in 1802, was regarded as a quintessential masterpiece of historic landscape, and although Turner did not join those gullible colleagues who in 1797 fell for the so-called 'Venetian Secret' – ostensibly a recipe for the technique of the great Venetian masters but in fact a mischievous hoax – the bold handling and contrasts of light and shade here can certainly be related to contemporary interest in Venetian painting. The unusual use of a pink ground was doubtless an experiment of Turner's own to achieve a comparably warm and resonant effect. No less significant an inspiration was probably Rembrandt, another master who was being looked at anew in the 1790s and by whom Turner had seen prints and drawings in the house of his friend and mentor Dr Monro, and a painting, 'Rest on the Flight into Egypt', when visiting his patron Sir Richard Colt Hoare at Stourhead. Most immediately, however, Turner was probably thinking back to Wilson, and to his dramatic deployment of figures in historic land-scapes. Turner's tours of Wales in the 1790s were pil-grimages to Wilson, and it was partly the recollection of Wilson's pictures that inspired Turner to intersperse sketches of historical subjects among his drawings of the scenery on his most ambitious Welsh tour in 1798.

The genesis of this picture is to be found in a pencil drawing in the *Dinevor Castle* sketchbook used that summer (TB XL 8 *verso*; D 01476), and the stormy mountainous landscape is evidently inspired by Wales. The drawing shows several figures, whereas only the one, lying on the ground apparently dead or wounded, appears in the painting; on f.73 of the same sketch-book, however, this figure appears again, accompanied by a woman (D 01585). These figures could be drawn from Welsh history, or perhaps allude to a classical story such as Ovid's tale of the tragic lovers Pyramus and Thisbe. Pyramus committed suicide beneath a mulberry tree after finding a scarf dropped by Thisbe as she ran away from a lioness; the animal, seizing the garment, had stained it with the blood of her last meal which was still around her mouth, but Pyramus believed his lover to be dead. Thisbe, on finding his body, likewise killed herself. The fruit of the tree turned from white to red with all this spilt blood. The subject had been magnificently treated by Poussin in his 'Landscape with Pyramus and Thisbe' then in the Ashburnham collection and now in the Städelsches Kunstinstitut, Frankfurt-am-Main. A few years later, in his notes for his Perspective Lectures at the Academy, Turner ranked this picture as a 'truly sub-lime' example of Poussin's 'abilities of Grandeur and pastoral subjects'.

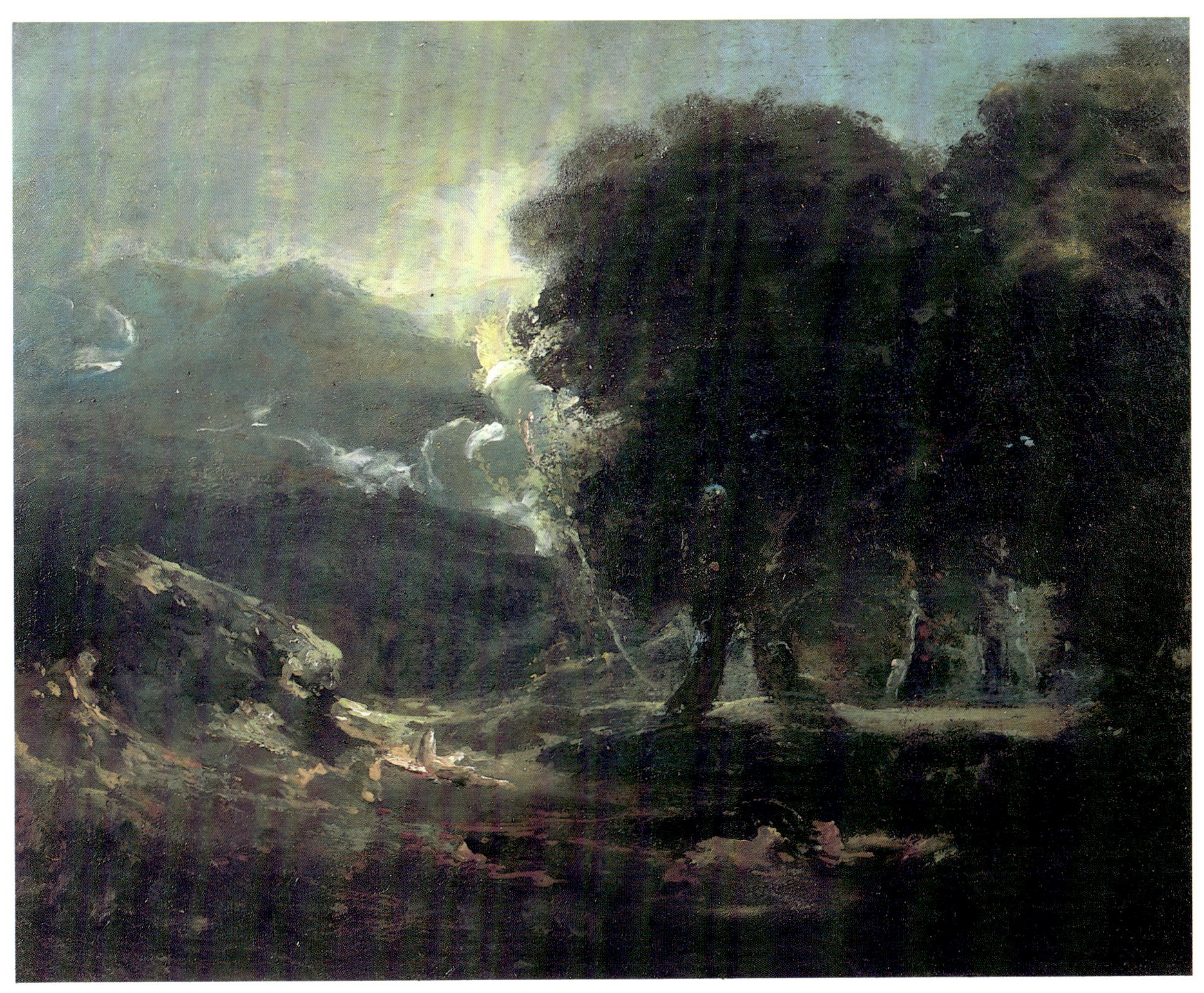

3   Aeneas and the Sibyl, Lake Avernus

*c.*1798

Oil on canvas 765 × 985 ($30\frac{1}{8}$ × $38\frac{3}{4}$)

N 00463

This, Turner's first completed essay in the tradition of classical and historic landscape evolved by Poussin and Claude and established in England by Wilson, was evidently painted at the instigation of Sir Richard Colt Hoare of Stourhead, an important patron of Turner by 1795. Colt Hoare was a man of wide classical culture whose gardens presented – as they still do today – a series of ideal vistas evocative of Claude's paintings. Among Colt Hoare's distinguished collection of pictures at Stourhead was one by Wilson traditionally supposed to show Lake Avernus, but subsequently discovered to represent Lake Nemi, with Diana and Callisto. Colt Hoare perhaps proposed the present subject to Turner in order to compensate for this change, as well as to encourage the painter to tackle a finished landscape with classical associations. Although there is no conclusive evidence that Colt Hoare specifically commissioned it, the theme was of special concern to him as the gardens at Stourhead, with their fine lake with grottoes and temples, had almost certainly been laid out by his grandfather Henry Hoare at least partly to recall the places visited by Aeneas on his epic wanderings from Troy to Latium, where be became the ancestral hero of the Romans, as recounted by Virgil in the *Aeneid*. Lake Avernus, which filled the crater of an extinct volcano near Cumae and Puteoli, features significantly in the story for nearby was the cave of the Cumaean Sibyl, through which Aeneas descended to the lower world. Henry Hoare's correspondence shows that he was aware of the parallels between his garden and the lake and cave as described by Virgil.

Turner's subject comes from the sixth book of the *Aeneid*. Here, Aeneas is told by the Cumaean Sibyl that he may enter the underworld, where he seeks the shade of his father, only if he carries a golden bough from a sacred tree as an offering to Proserpine. Turner based the composition on a drawing of the lake made by Colt Hoare on 4 February 1786; Colt Hoare describes the subject of his 'correct' sketch as follows: 'the Lake of Avernus in the foreground, with the temple on its banks; above it is the *Monte nuovo*, which was thrown up by a volcanic force in one night. In the next distance are the Lucrine Lake, beyond it the castle of Baiae, and the lofty promontory of Misenum, with the island of Capri at the extremity of the horizon.' A further drawing, in the Turner Bequest (TB LI N; D 02381), shows a related composition, with the addition of antique masonry in the foreground but without figures. It is not by Turner, nor, apparently, by Colt Hoare, but it too probably helped to form the painting since the masonry is retained in the latter. The story of Aeneas was a recurrent theme in Turner's work. Between 1814 and 1815 he repeated this subject, this time definitely for Colt Hoare, who hung it as a companion to the Wilson of Lake Nemi; this second version is now at the Yale Center for British Art, New Haven (B & J 226). If Colt Hoare ever owned the version in the Bequest, he must have returned it. While the Bequest picture is still very Wilsonian, the Yale version is closer in spirit to Claude.

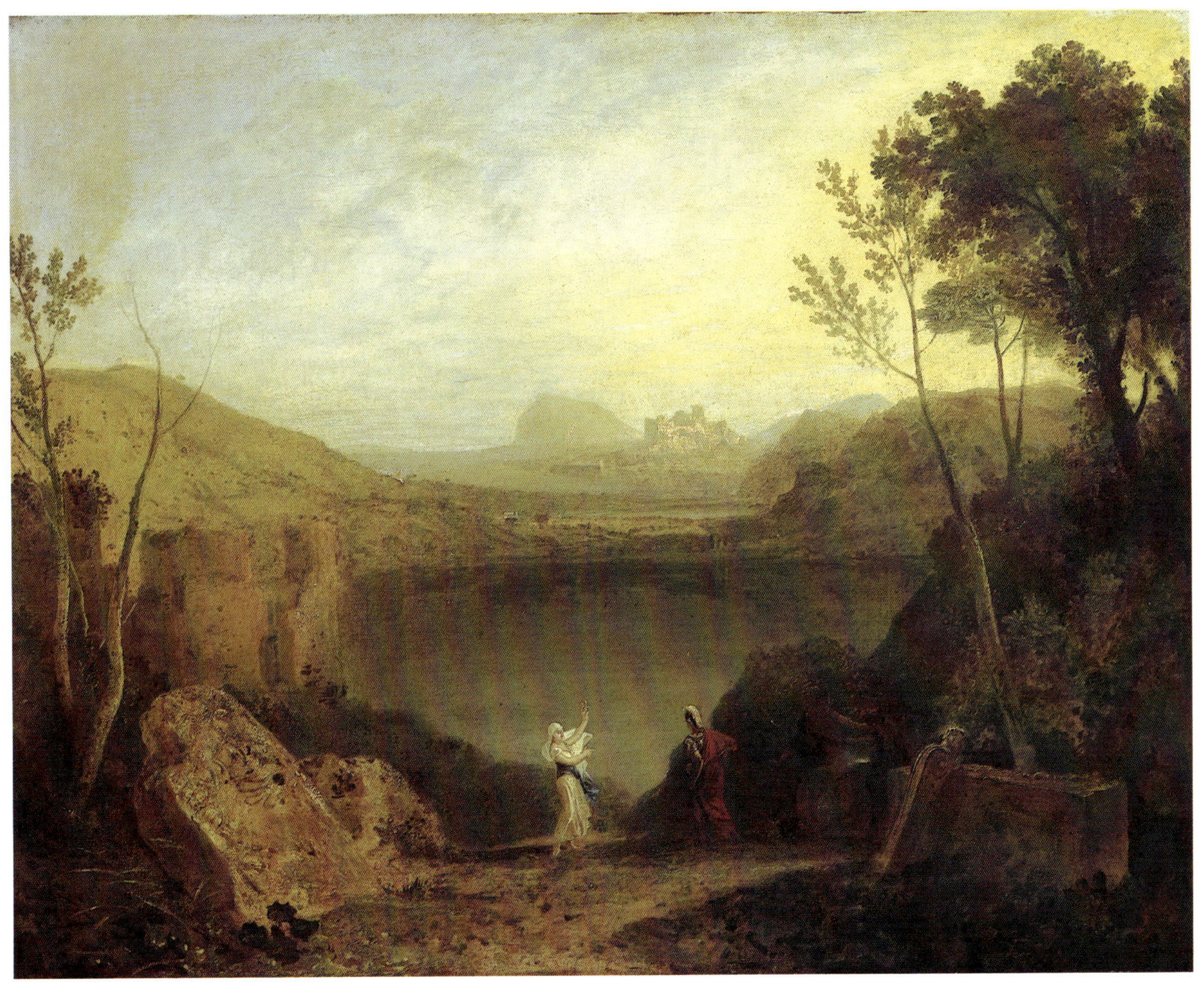

4   **Landscape with Lake and Fallen Tree**

?c.1800

Oil on canvas 390 × 605 (15⅜ × 23⅞)

N 03557

Evidently a 'lay in' for a small picture left unfinished by Turner, this is notable for its brighter colour. A higher colour key is a feature of his work in oil by 1800, and is particularly marked in studies of trees or pure landscape. In other aspects however this picture still recalls Wilson, and the naked figure with raised leg, like that in cat.no.2, may indicate that Turner was working towards an historic subject. Such figures were a staple of Turner's studies in the life class at the Royal Academy, and can also be found in Wilson's work, particularly in the foreground of his early historic landscape 'The Destruction of Niobe's Children'. Turner's study is in fact so close to the structure of that composition in the prime version formerly in the National Gallery and destroyed in the last war, as to have been perhaps provoked by it, though it lacks most of the 'Sublime' features introduced by Wilson. There is no storm or cataract, and only the one figure instead of the suffering group in the foreground; however, the curious darker blur at the upper left may approximate to Wilson's cloud bearing Apollo and Diana. Wilson's 'Niobe' was an archetype of historic landscape. Reynolds had criticised it in his fourteenth *Discourse* to the Academy for an uneasy blend of epic drama and a natural setting 'too near common nature', but most critics regarded it highly. In the early 1790s, the picture belonged to the Academy's Keeper, the sculptor Joseph Wilton; it was then sold to the influential connoisseur Sir George Beaumont, who praised Wilson for his 'elevation of thought and dignity of composition'. The picture was also widely celebrated through the magnificent engraving made by William Woollett in 1761 – one of four prints after Wilson which were later to serve as the standard of excellence Turner hoped to match in large plates engraved after his own paintings. When contemplating four engravings from his pictures, on the same ambitious scale as Woollett's, in 1822, he wrote to his publisher J.O. Robinson: 'to succeed would perhaps form another epoch in the English school; and, if we fall, we fall by contending with giant strength'.

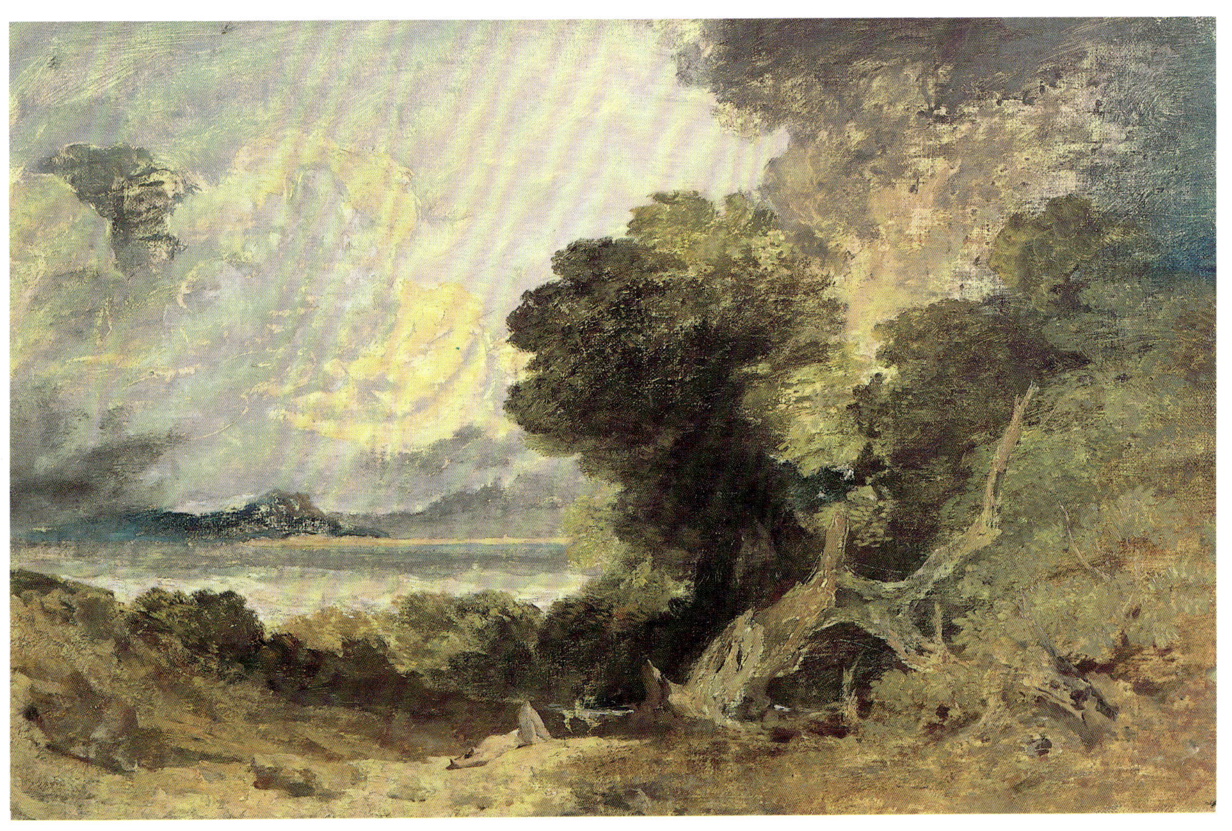

5   **Mountain Scene: ?Martigny with the Castle of La Bâtiaz** *c.*1802–3

Oil on canvas 440 × 540 ($17\frac{1}{4}$ × $21\frac{1}{4}$)

N 00465

Though still belonging to Turner's Wilsonian phase, this small but finished picture has also something of the wild bleakness of Salvator Rosa, whose 'savage' landscape style represented the opposite extreme from the classicism of Poussin or Claude, and had done much to form the current taste for the 'Sublime'. Turner's most developed essay in Rosa's manner was the dark and broken landscape setting of 'Jason' (N 00471; B & J 19), exhibited at the Academy in 1802 just before Turner's departure for Switzerland and Paris.

Until recently this picture has been considered to be a view in Wales, based most probably on his 1798 tour; indeed it has been connected with sketches in the *Dinevor Castle* and *Dolbadarn* sketchbooks used that year or shortly afterwards, and also has much in common with some watercolours supposedly of Welsh castles. However, the background mountains seem too massive and jagged for Wales and the scene is more probably Martigny, in the Rhône valley, with the ruined castle of La Bâtiaz, a fortress of the bishops of Sion, dismantled in 1518. Turner visited Martigny in 1802 and made several drawings, chiefly in the series known as the *Grenoble* sketchbook (TB LXXIV). A more effective comparison is the view engraved by W.B. Cooke for Roger's *Italy*, from the watercolour Turner developed from these earlier drawings in about 1827 (TB CCLXXX 154; D 27671).

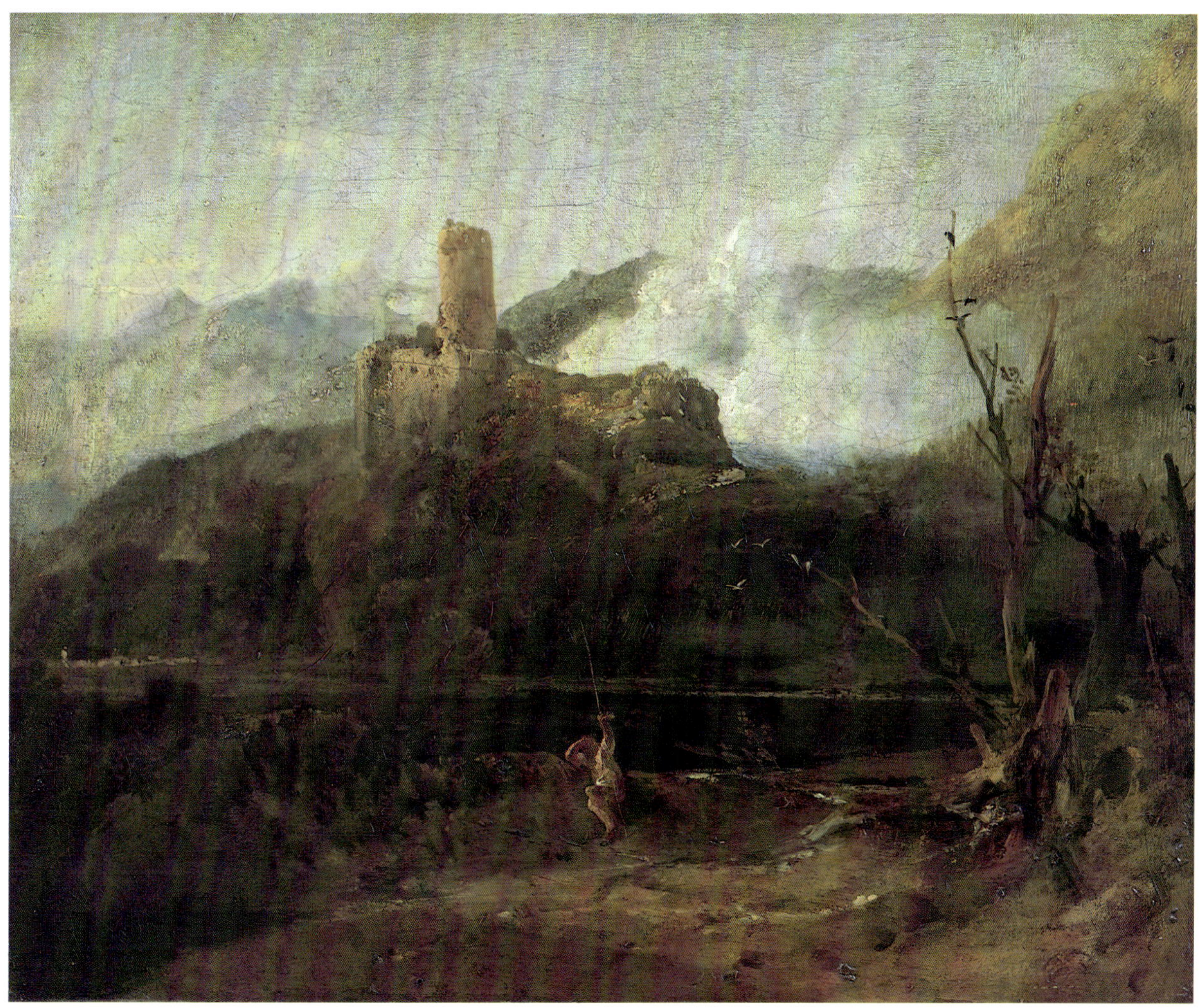

6 Margate, Setting Sun *c*.1806–7

Oil on canvas 855 × 1162 (33¾ × 45¾)

N 02700

One of a group of seventeen sketches in the Bequest of similarly large size, mainly of Thames subjects, all of which are loosely painted over a chalky ground and some of which Turner may have begun out-of-doors. He may have worked on rolls of canvas, as he did later at Cowes in 1827 and in Italy in 1828.

Turner's interest in coast and marine subjects went back to his earliest days as a painter, but became especially pronounced in the first decade of the new century. Between 1807 and 1809 he painted a number of pictures of shipping in the Thames estuary, and also treated coastal subjects either in the tradition of the Dutch masters of the seventeenth century, as in the case of 'The Sun Rising through Vapour', exhibited in 1807 (National Gallery; B & J 69), or based on his own very specific studies of the scenery and activities of the shores of England as in 'St Mawes at the Pilchard Season' shown in 1812 (N 00484; B & J 123). Turner's concern for the English coast was at least partly a patriotic one, for the integrity of the maritime frontier was of course crucially important in the war against Napoleonic France.

Margate, on the North Foreland, had particular associations for Turner. In about 1786 he had been sent there to stay with relatives of his mother, and attended Mr Coleman's school; then also he had made some precocious drawings of the town including one that contained his earliest depiction of seagoing ships. Probably between 1801 and 1803 Turner painted his first oil of Margate and its old pier (Gaskell Collection; B & J 51), and between 1806 and 1809 he made a series of pencil sketches of the town in his *River and Margate* sketchbook (TB XCIX). Later, in the 1830s and up to 1847, he visited the town frequently to stay with his friend Mrs Booth. By then Margate had grown from a small fishing community into a bustling seaside resort, its bay lined with stucco houses and its beach with bathing machines, and visited by crowds of Londoners who were transported there by packet steamers; in 1806 and 1807 these developments were just beginning, and visitors like Turner, if they did not make the journey by road, were brought, crowded together and often seasick, in the Margate hoy. This large sketch shows the range of activities that might have greeted them as they arrived at the jetty on a fine evening, and perhaps anticipates the kind of detailed account of a fishing port that Turner gave in 'St Mawes' a few years later.

A finished picture showing Margate from much the same viewpoint but from further offshore, and in breezy morning conditions, was exhibited in Turner's gallery in 1808; then, or subsequently, it was bought by Lord Egremont and is still at Petworth (B & J 78). In this sketch, with its serene evening sunlight, suggestive of the glowing atmospheric treatments of the Dutch painter, Aelbert Cuyp, Turner was perhaps thinking towards a picture of contrasted effects.

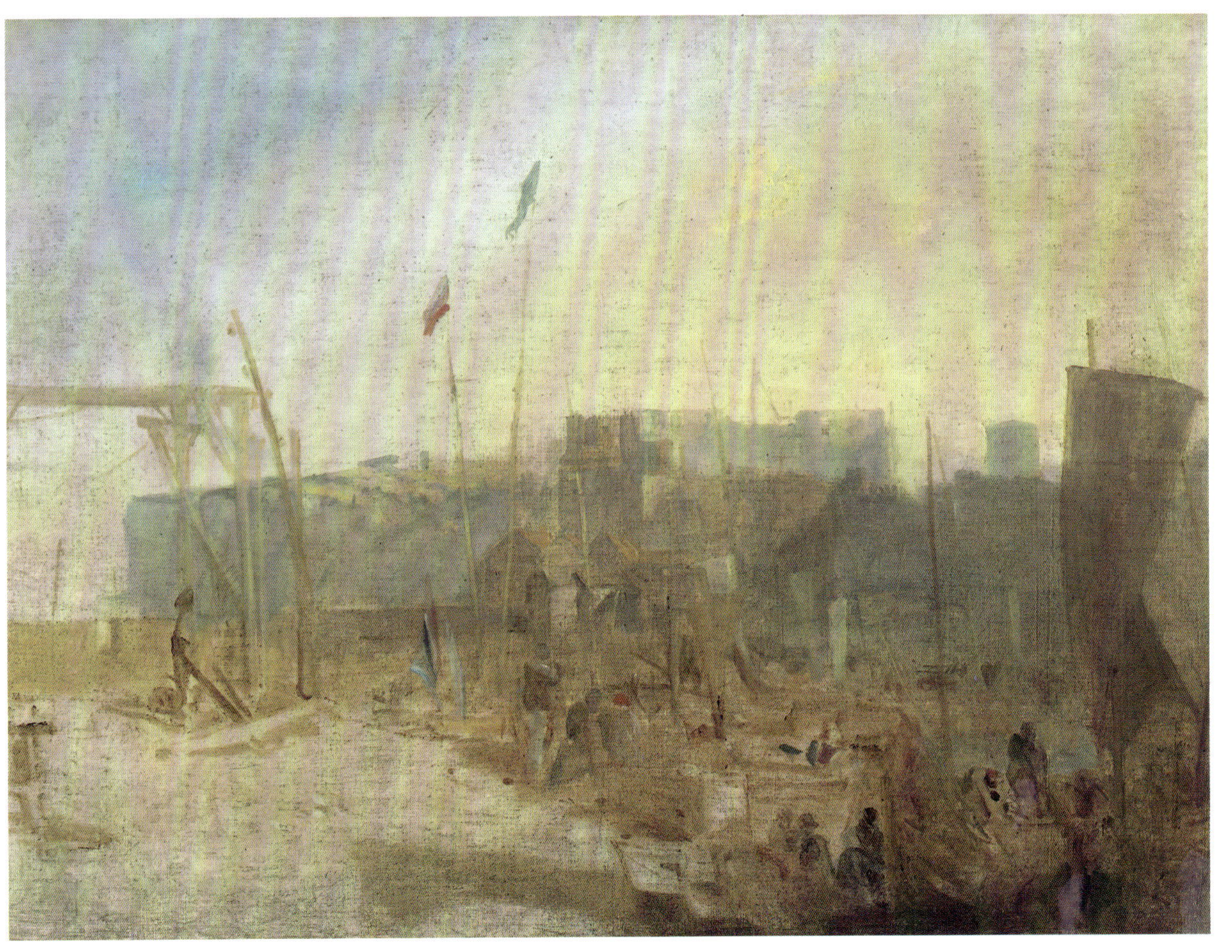

7   Shipping at the Mouth of the Thames

*c.*1806–7

Oil on canvas 860 × 1170 (33¾ × 46)

N 02702

This is one of the most fully developed, and most beautiful, of the large oil sketches on loose canvas made about 1806 or 1807. It is also one of those most closely related to the compositions and subjects of his finished work of the period, and could have been quite readily worked up to exhibition finish. From 1807, Turner exhibited a series of pictures in his own gallery of shipping in the Thames estuary. The Nore, where the Thames and the Medway converged off Sheerness to form the busiest and most important naval and commercial anchorage in Britain, was a subject rich in inspiration to a lover of the sea like Turner, but its significance was all the more widely appreciated in time of war. In his paintings of this great waterway, where wave-tossed fishing boats or small craft are characteristically juxtaposed with the reassuring presence of the navy, Turner was both expressing and appealing to a sense of patriotism and national identity. The formula here is essentially that of the finished pictures, and as in most of them, Sheerness seems visible on the shoreline in the distance. The cool sunlight slanting from the cloud and playing over the waves seems perfectly spontaneous and natural, almost as if studied from nature, but although Turner may well have begun other sketches out-of-doors about this time, he could hardly have handled a substantial canvas in a boat in windy weather.

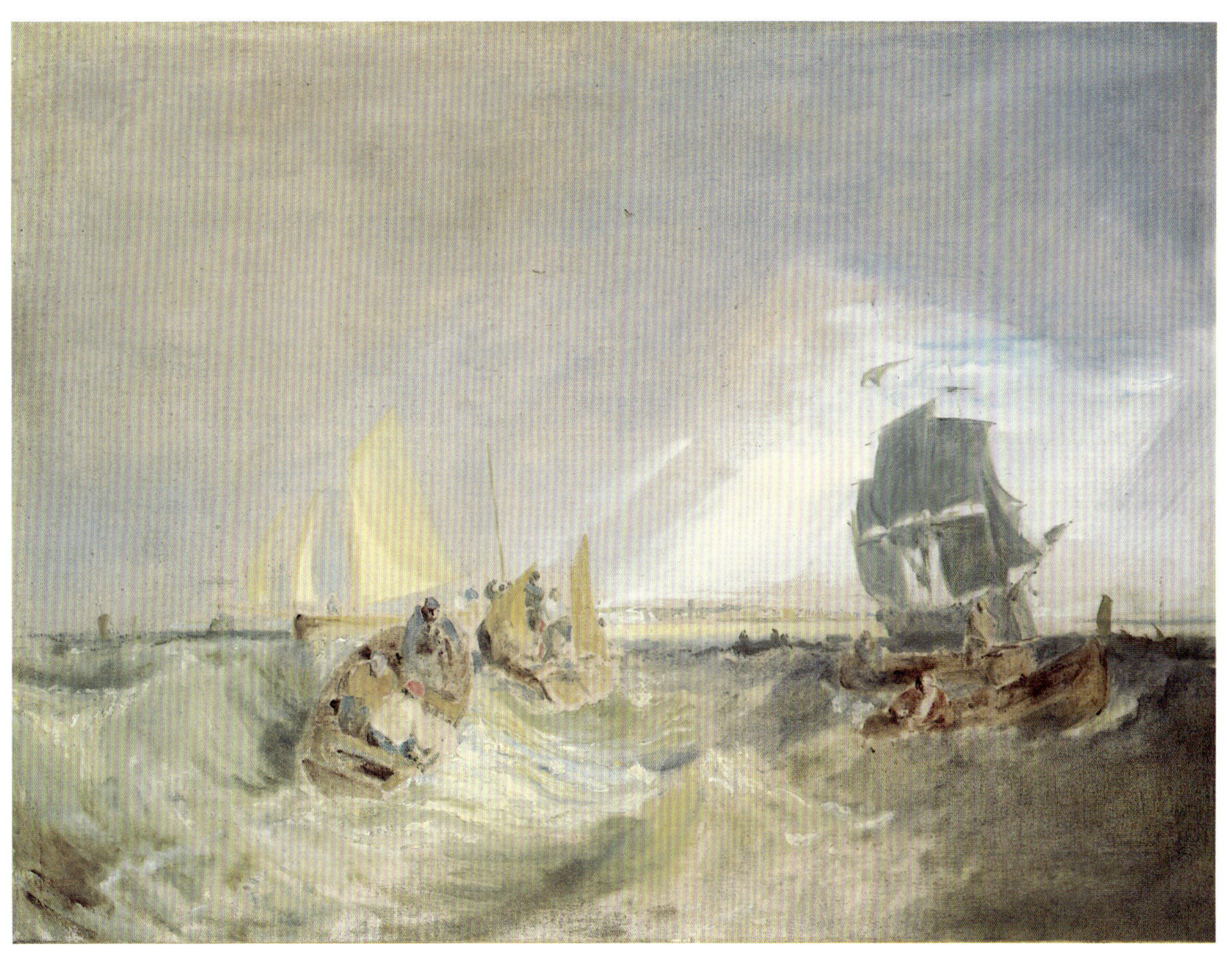

8   **Goring Mill and Church** *c.*1806–7

Oil on canvas 855 × 1160 (33¾ × 45¾)

N 02704

The majority of the large sketches on loose canvas made in about 1806 or 1807 are of scenes on the Thames west of London. From May 1805 Turner had a second home at Isleworth, and late the following year he moved to a house in Upper Mall, Hammersmith, which he kept as his escape from central London until 1811. His affection for this stretch of the Thames was sustained when in 1813 he completed his cottage at Twickenham. According to the son of his friend and fishing companion the Revd Henry Trimmer, Turner 'had a boat at Richmond ... From his boat he painted on a large canvas direct from Nature. Till you have seen these sketches, you know nothing of Turner's powers. There are about two score of these large subjects'. Trimmer's remarks evidently refer to the series to which this sketch belongs, and are the strongest evidence we have that some were at least begun out-of-doors; certainly it is rather easier to believe this tradition of sketches like this than it is in the case of the previous example. On the other hand the degree of completion in some passages in this picture, contrasted to the absence of work on the foreground, probably suggests a more schematic and considered studio process. Turner can be seen to have worked over a white ground to achieve a bright and translucent effect, anticipating the atmospheric unity through light that distinguishes many of his finished pictures – including those of Thames scenery – of a few years later.

A different view of Goring church occurs on f.19 of the *Thames from Reading to Walton* sketchbook used when Turner was exploring the river in about 1806 (TB XCV; D 05923). Besides these drawings and his large sketches on canvas, Turner also made a series of eighteen smaller oil sketches on mahogany panels of scenes on the Thames and its tributary, the Wey (N 02302– 02313, N 02676–02681; B&J 177–94). These are likewise very fresh and spontaneous, and may well have been painted out-of-doors. Despite their small size, they share with their larger counterparts on canvas Turner's consistent habit of thinking pictorially; however slight their execution, the sketches are always resolved compositionally and are not altogether to be compared with the immediacy of Constable's 'natural painture'. However, they are symptomatic of a major shift in Turner's response to nature away from the historic 'Sublime' or the formally classical, and towards a more subtle, atmospheric and distinctly English pastoral.

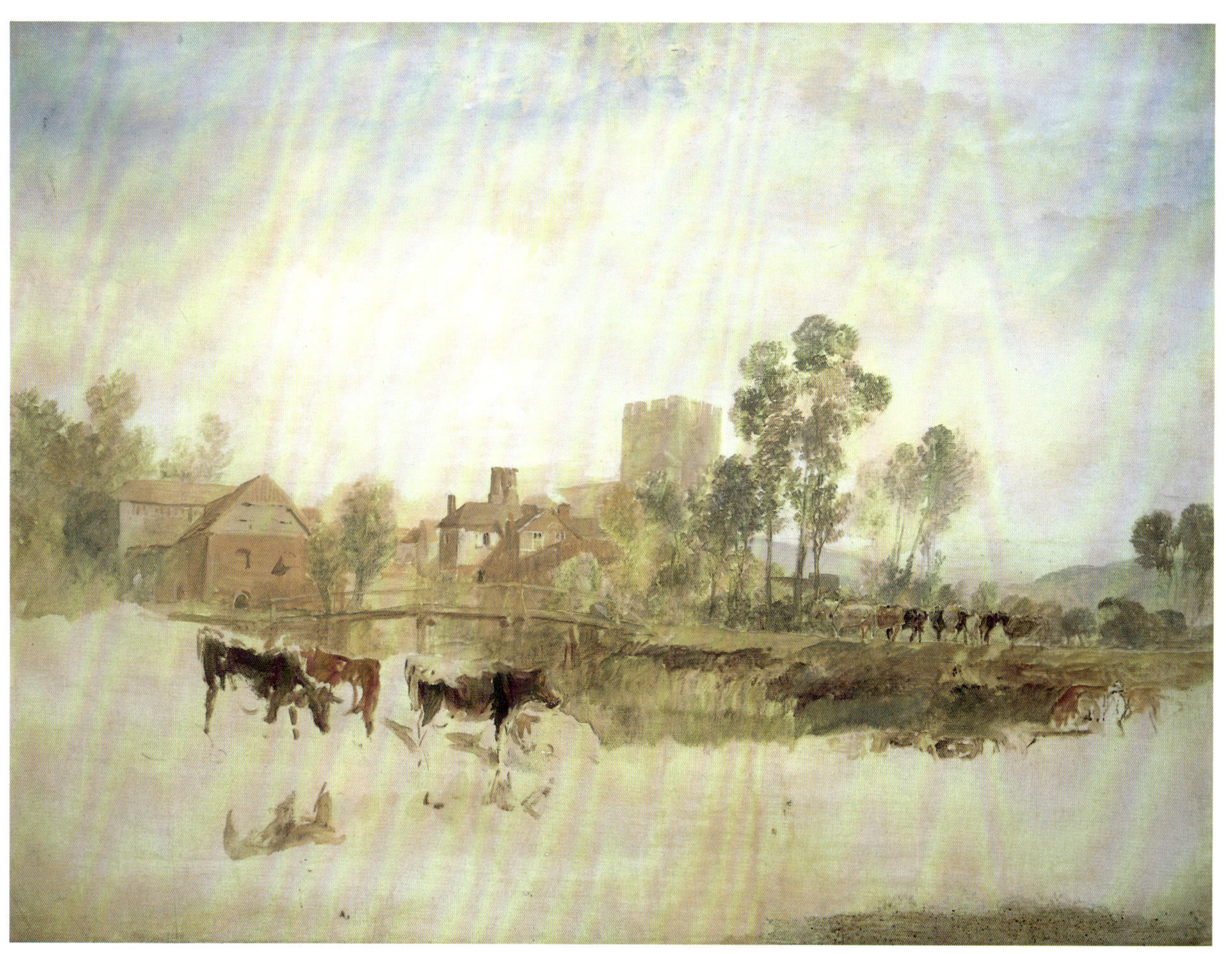

9   **Fishing upon the Blythe-Sand, Tide
Setting In** Exh. 1809

Oil on canvas 890 × 1195 (35 × 47)

N 00496

This beautifully simple coast scene, with its almost
abstract pattern of horizontal and diagonal planes and
shifting lights, represents a finished treatment of the
kind of Thames subjects Turner essayed rather earlier
in his large oil sketches like cat.no.7. It has particularly
been related to a coast scene with figures and boats on
the sands in the foreground and a different arrangement of the ships (N 02698; B & J 176), but the similari-
ties are probably coincidental. A wash drawing,
likewise in the Bequest (TB CXX Q; D 08231), also has
points in common. Blyth Sands look across to Canvey
Island, above Sheerness.

The picture was frequently exhibited by Turner,
firstly in his own gallery in 1809, then again in 1810, at
the Royal Academy in 1815 as 'Bligh Sand, near Sheerness: Fishing Boats Trawling', and at Plymouth later

that year, as confirmed by a letter written by Turner to
the artist Ambrose Johns on 4 November. It was still
available when Turner wrote to his patron Sir John
Leicester on 12 December the following year, offering
it for sale with three others including 'The Sun Rising
through Vapour'; his letter included a pen sketch of the
composition. According to Thornbury, Turner had the
'proud pleasure' of refusing to sell the picture to Sir
George Beaumont, the patron, collector and amateur
artist who had been a virulent and influential critic of
his work since at least 1803, when he had likened the
white spray and turbulent sea in 'Calais Pier' (National
Gallery; B & J 48) to 'veins in a marble slab' and 'pease
soup'. Beaumont, whose taste was inclined to be con-
servative, found Turner's colouring artificial and often
too pale, and his execution sometimes coarse, but this
picture could have struck him as avoiding some of
these failings, and he may well have hoped to heal his
breach with the artist, whom he claimed he 'personally
liked'. Turner retained the picture but took little care
of it, even, according to one nearly contemporary
story, using it as a cat door.

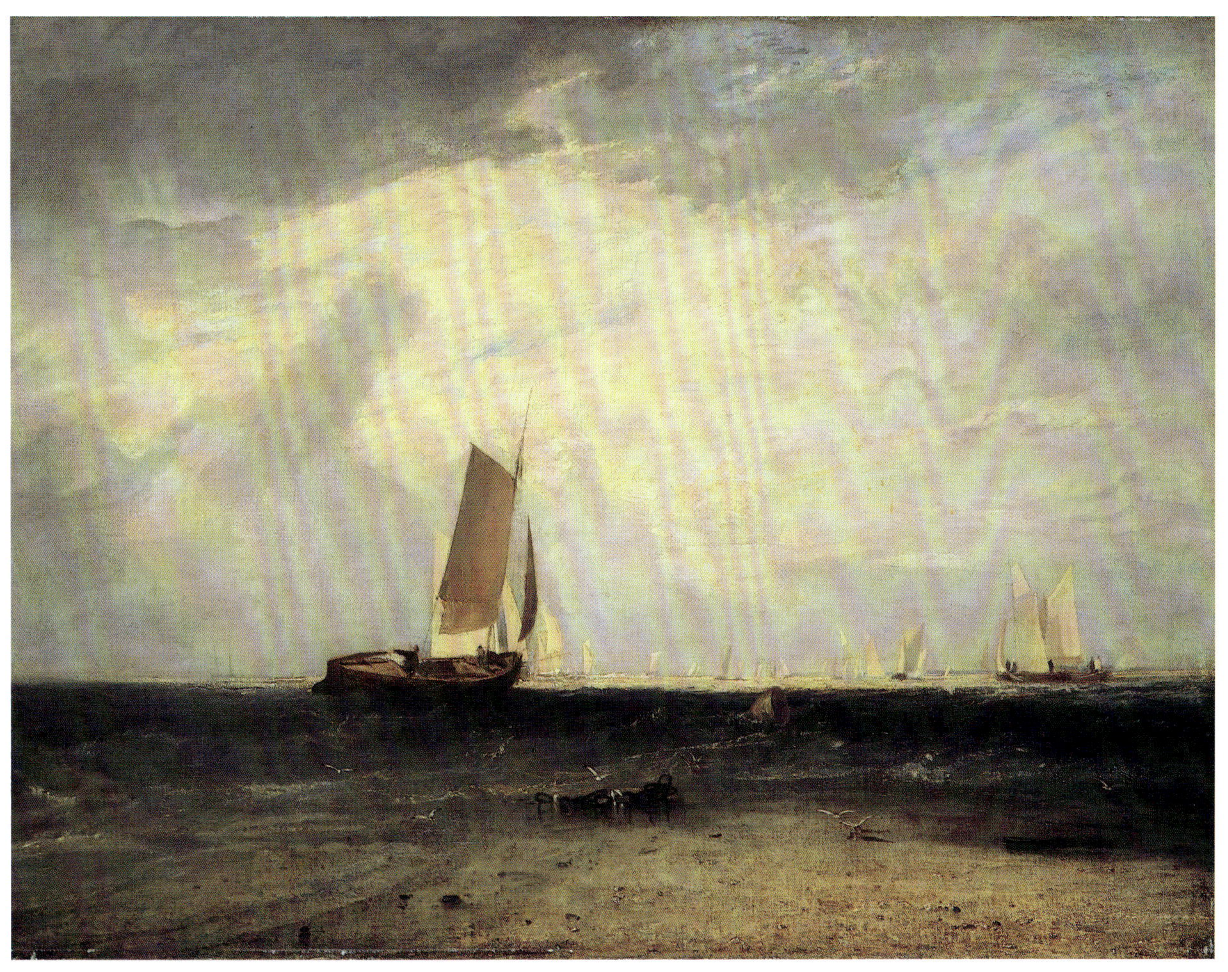

10   **Sketch of a Bank with Gypsies**

?Exh. 1809

Oil on canvas 615 × 840 (24⅛ × 33)

N 00467

This is a finished picture and was very probably the work of the above title exhibited in Turner's gallery in 1809. Between 1815 and 1820 the composition was etched by Turner himself in soft-ground and again – uniquely – with the addition of aquatint, for the *Liber Studiorum*. The plate was never published, but would have fallen into the 'Pastoral' category of the *Liber*. The *Liber* was intended to proclaim the wide variety of subject matter Turner was now embracing, and 'Pastoral' itself comprehended a range of landscape types running from ideal and classical subjects descended from Claude, to robustly rustic scenes like this, which deploy all the ingredients of the contemporary taste for the 'Picturesque'. Derived from Dutch painters of the seventeenth century and from the largely imaginary landscape inventions of Gainsborough, and popularised by the writings of arbiters of taste like Uvedale Price, Richard Payne Knight and the Revd William Gilpin, the 'Pictur-

esque' concentrated on a rough and deliberately inelegant vocabulary of contrasted textures and lights, uneven forms, broken trees or posts; and gypsies were of course the appropriate inhabitants of such rugged landscapes. Turner's 'Sketch', with its gypsies resting by a fire in a hollow, its cattle and slanted post, its chiaroscuro and its contrast between natural and artificial light, was undoubtedly intended as a definitive statement of this taste, and in describing it as a 'Sketch' while finishing it for exhibition he was alluding to another aspect of the convention – a preference for vigorous and spontaneous handling and broken paint textures. The motif of the figures by the fire, set in deep shadow, shows Turner's continuing involvement with the art of Rembrandt, and an echo of the similar group of the Holy Family in the master's 'Flight into Egypt' that he had seen at Stourhead (see cat.no.2). Similarly 'Picturesque' features occur independently in the contemporary work of young artists like William Mulready and John Crome; while Turner's friend and admirer Augustus Wall Callcott, whose early work was strongly inclined to the 'Picturesque', probably used the 'Sketch' as the model for his own 'Travelling Tinkers' (Osborne House), exhibited in 1811.

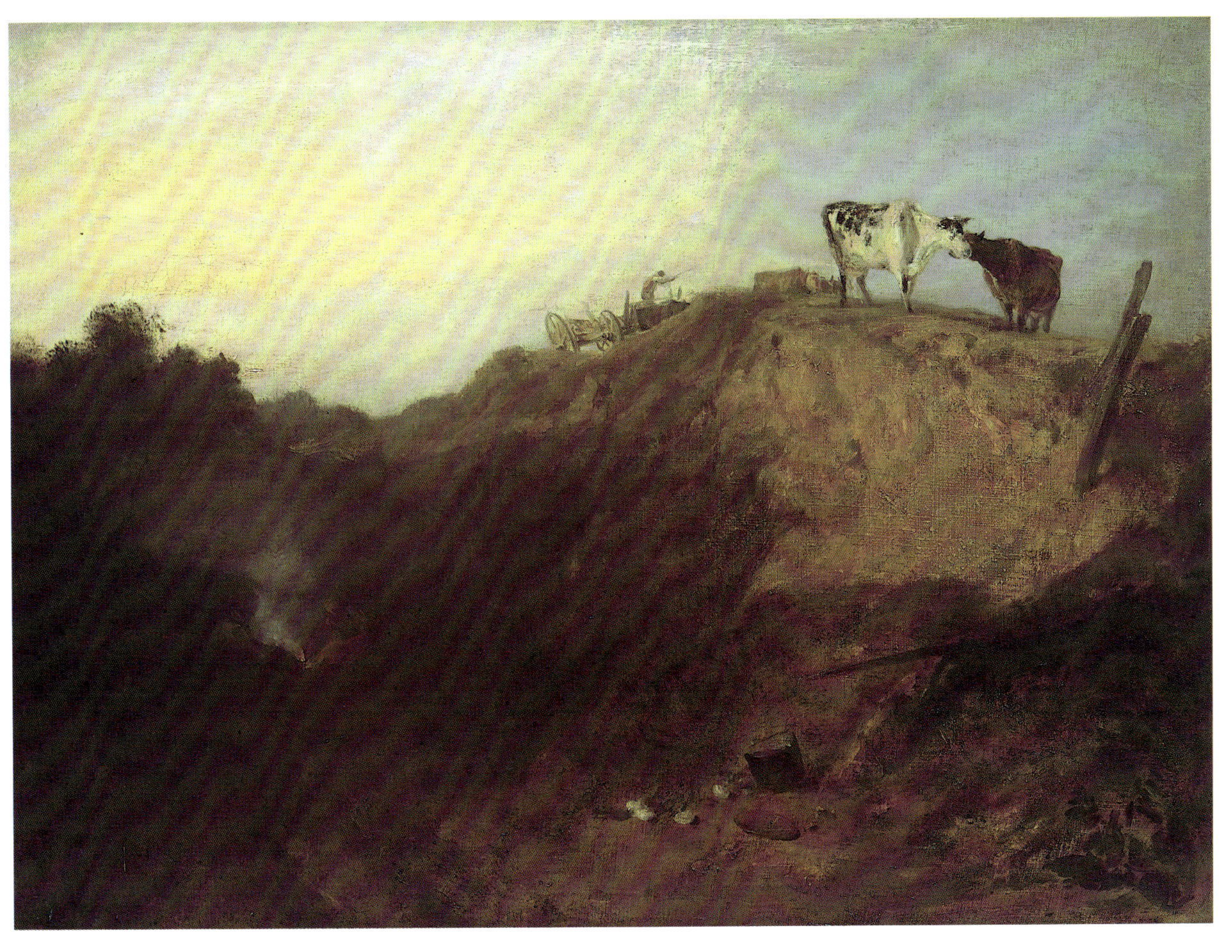

11 The Plym Estuary from Boringdon Park 1813

Oil on prepared paper 245 × 305 ($9\frac{5}{8}$ × 12)
TB CXXX E; D02911

In the summer of 1813 Turner paid his second visit to Devonshire, where he spent some time in the Plymouth area with friends including the journalist Cyrus Redding, the local artist Ambrose Johns, and another painter, Charles Lock Eastlake, who had been born in Devon and was the pupil of the historical painter Benjamin Robert Haydon whose family came from Plymouth. On this holiday Turner pursued a new campaign of oil sketching in the open air, though now on a much smaller scale than he had used for his canvas sketches painted along the Thames and Wey a few years earlier (see cat.no.8). The spur, according to Eastlake, came from Johns, who 'fitted up a small portable painting-box, containing some prepared paper for oil sketches'. When Turner paused to sketch, Johns 'produced the inviting box, and the great artist, finding everything ready to his hand, immediately began to work … and after a few days he made his oil sketches freely in our presence'. Turner apparently enjoyed the speed with which he could paint them, and 'himself remarked that one of these sketches (and perhaps the best) was done in less than half an hour'. Eastlake also records that Turner later declared that his Devon sketches had become 'worthless, in consequence, as he supposed of some defects in the preparation of the paper'; all the grey tints, he observed, had nearly 'disappeared'. This deterioration is not apparent in this vivid and sparkling work, which approaches more nearly than the Thames sketches to the spirit of Constable's sketches from nature. It is twice the size of the other fifteen Devon sketches, which were presumably painted on similar sheets of paper split in half; the paper seems to have been of a heavy grade, prepared on one side with an oil medium.

Eastlake's account notwithstanding, there is some doubt as to whether Turner's Devon sketches were necessarily all made from nature, and a comparison of this example with the actual place shows Turner taking considerable liberties with topography. Nevertheless, the main features are identifiable. Turner was evidently working from a vantage point not far from the south gate of Boringdon Park – Redding recalled that Lord Boringdon was one of the 'discriminating friends of the fine arts' who entertained him in Devon – looking towards the Long Bridge over the Plym and the estuary beyond. The building on the hill at right is a fort then known as Clarke's Battery. The low tide, bright afternoon sun and freshly harvested fields indicate a time in late August or early September 1813.

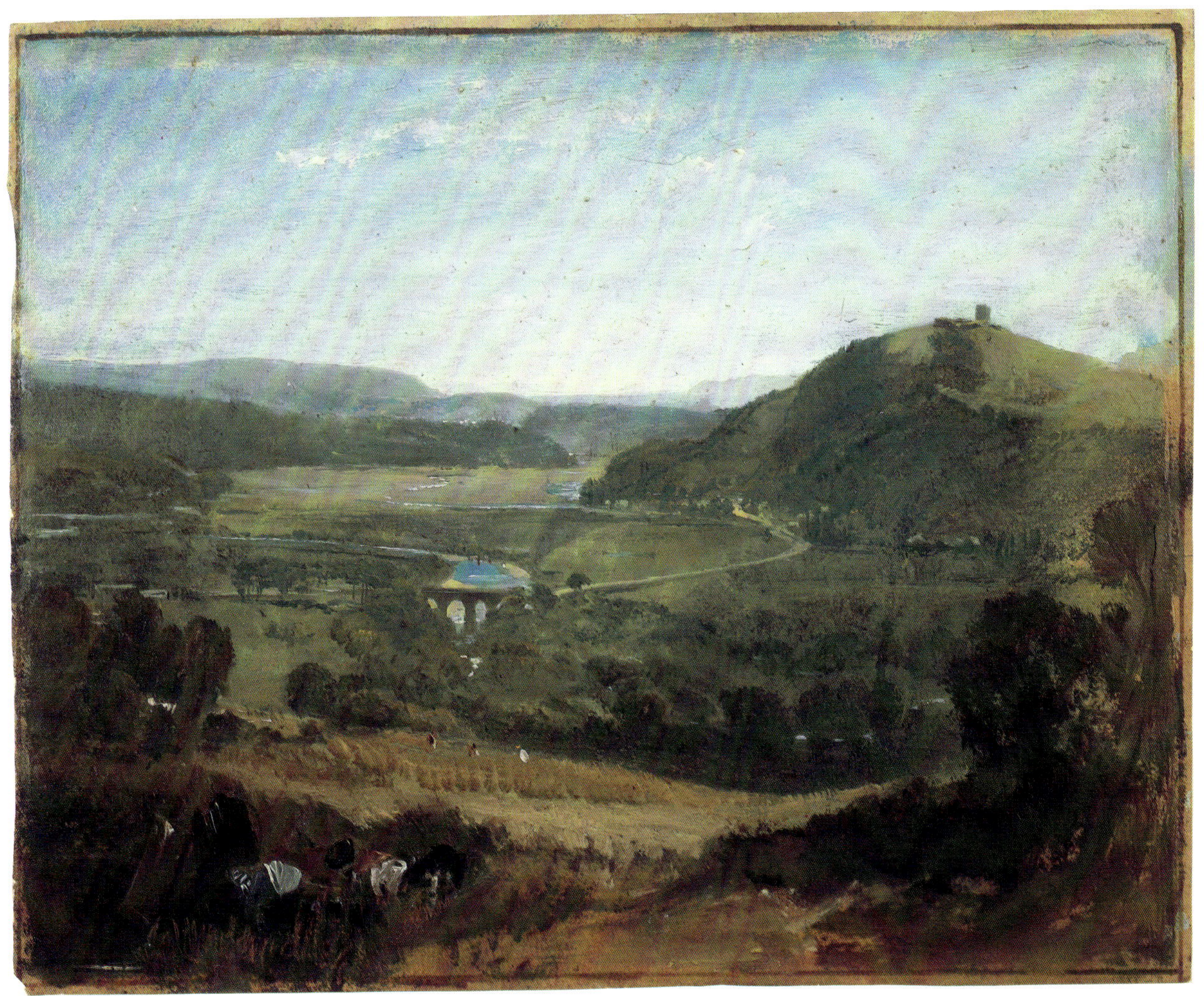

12   Death on a Pale Horse *c.*1825–30

Oil on canvas 600 × 755 ($23\frac{1}{2}$ × $29\frac{3}{4}$)

N 05504

The subject and status of this picture are not entirely certain. Its very liquid paint and curious combination of rubbing and scratching, are unique in Turner's work in oil, although these features correspond closely to his practice in watercolour. The image is macabre and visionary, and seems to spring from some inner crisis of the artist's rather than, perhaps, to provide a foundation for a finished picture. Nevertheless it shows that Turner's early interest in subjects of the historical 'Sublime' was sustained into his mid career, and anticipates the apocalyptic pictures he was to paint in the 1840s. The subject has most often been identified as 'Death on a Pale Horse' from the sixth chapter of the Book of Revelation:

> And I looked, and behold a pale horse;
> and his name that sat on him was Death,
> and Hell followed with him. And power was
> given unto them over the fourth part of
> the earth, to kill with sword, and with
> hunger, and with death, and with beasts of
> the earth.

The subject had been a major preoccupation of British Romantic artists. John Hamilton Mortimer was the author of a celebrated composition etched in 1784; William Blake and Turner's early mentor P.J. de Loutherbourg had addressed the theme; and most celebrated of all were Benjamin West's various pictures of it, beginning with works exhibited in 1784 and 1796 painted in connection with a project for a series of subjects from the Book of Revelation intended for King George III's chapel at Windsor. Turner had seen the 1796 version (Detroit Institute of Arts) exhibited in the Louvre in 1802, and again, no doubt, at the British Institution in 1806; later he was familiar with it in Lord Egremont's collection at Petworth, for which it had been acquired by 1820. In 1817 West had shown a very large finished version (now in the Pennsylvania Academy of the Fine Arts) in a special gallery at 125 Pall Mall, and after the painter's death in 1820 it hung with others of his most celebrated pictures in the gallery which his sons opened to the public on the site of his former home and studio in Newman Street. It might be tempting to see this obviously very personal work as in some sense a posthumous tribute to West, but it was probably painted up to a decade later and it has been suggested that Turner's motivation was the death of his father in 1829.

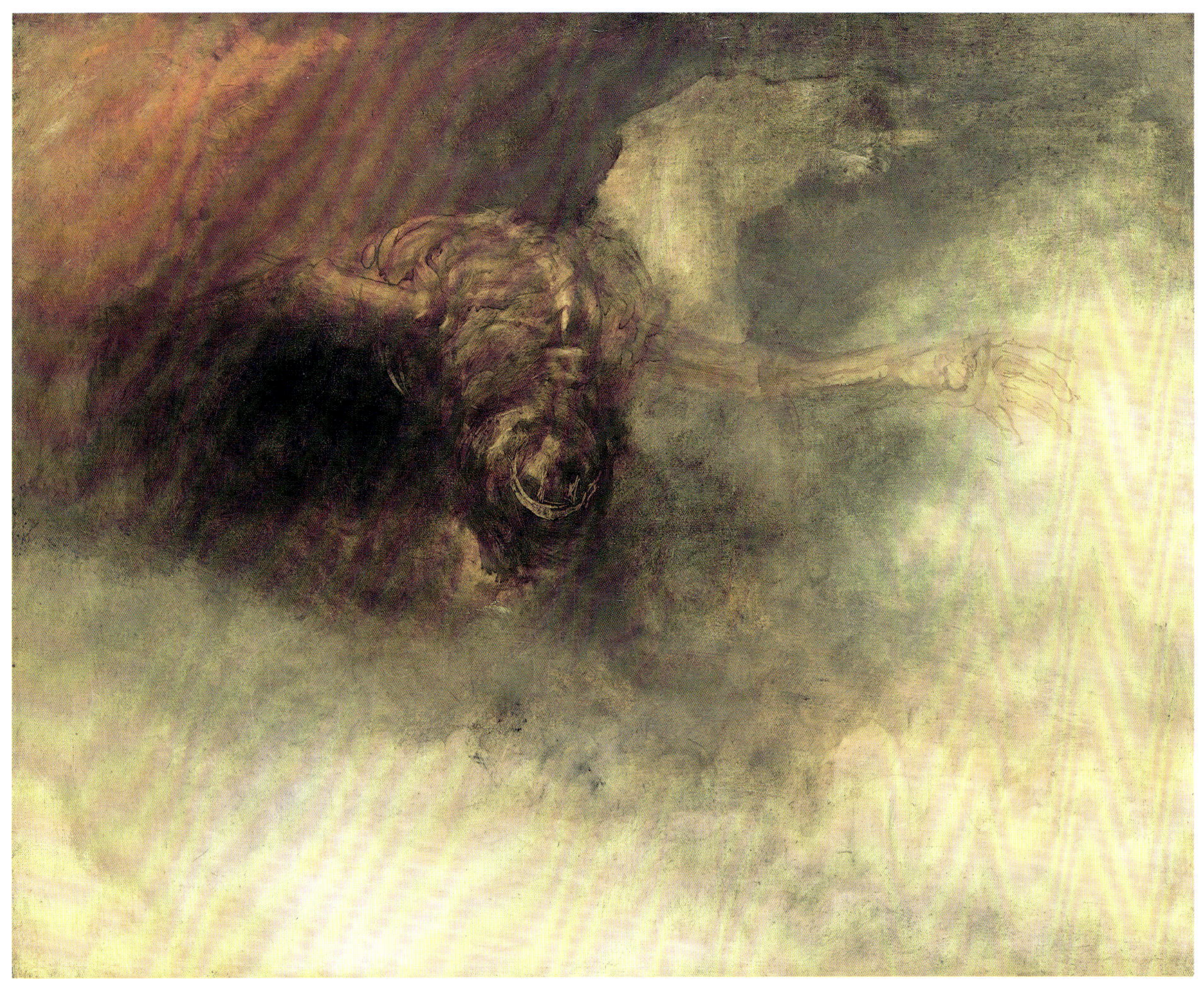

13 Evening Landscape, ?Chichester Canal

c.1825–8

Oil on canvas 650 × 1260 ($25\frac{1}{2}$ × $49\frac{1}{2}$)
Presented by Miss M.H. Turner, 1944
N 05563

This picture, unidentified in the schedule of the Turner Bequest, was presumably among the works in Turner's possession at his death but subsequently handed over to his next-of-kin as not being by the artist. It is however clearly by Turner, and its colouring and technique, involving thick paint worked over while still wet, seems to belong to the mid 1820s. The picture is usually associated with Turner's 'Chichester Canal' (B & J 290), one of four wide, horizontal landscapes, all of which were supposedly painted in 1828 and 1829 for the panelled dining room at Petworth; it has been considered an adjunct to the less finished version of the Petworth picture, in the Turner Bequest (N 00560; B & J 285). Chichester Canal, and its more important parent waterway, the Portsmouth and Arundel Canal, was a speculative investment of Lord Egremont's. He had offered substantial guarantees against the cost of the project, but it proved a failure and by 1826 he had withdrawn from it, incurring heavy losses. Thus there may well be grounds for dating at least the Chichester subject rather earlier than the other pictures for the dining room, since Lord Egremont would hardly have wished to be reminded of his expensive error of judgement. This sketch, from the mid 1820s, would on technical grounds thus be of the right date to connect with the Chichester pictures.

On the other hand there are some important differences from the others; there is no sign of Chichester Cathedral, and the peaked hills on the horizon are more distinctive and marked than the gently rounded hills in the other two paintings. There is some similarity to an earlier watercolour, of about 1815, of York Minster from the River Ouse (Private Collection; W 275), but again there is no such architectural feature to be found here and the points of resemblance consist in no more than the general aspects of water and bank. The one distinctive feature of this sketch appears to be a divide in the waterway at left as if into some tributary stream. The most that can really be said is that Turner may have projected this general design of a broad riverscape or canal scene into his more specific Chichester subject painted later for Petworth. This certainly could have been done in the case of the lighting effects, for both the Petworth and Bequest versions retain the sunset painted here; in these pictures the sunset is an anomaly since it would have to be taking place to the north, over the ridge of the South Downs.

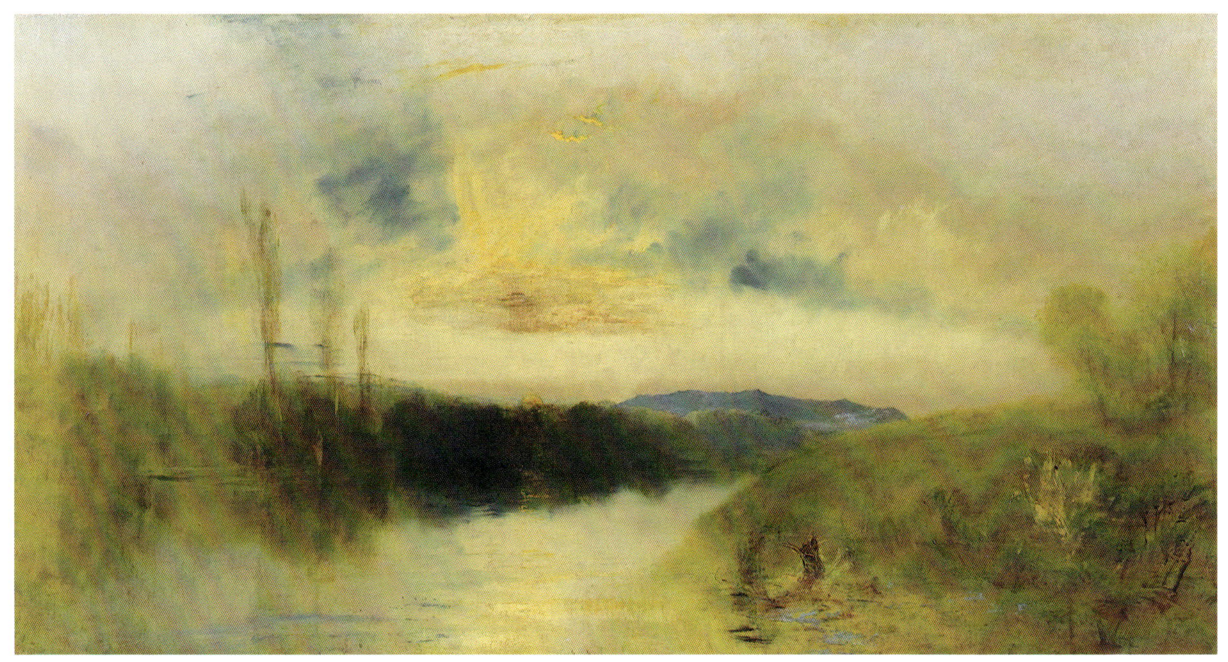

14 **Sketch for 'East Cowes Castle, the Regatta Beating to Windward'** 1827

Oil on canvas 465 × 720 (18¼ × 28½)

N 01993

In late July and August 1827, Turner stayed with the architect John Nash at East Cowes Castle on the Isle of Wight. This visit provoked an outburst of oil sketching which served for the two pictures commissioned by Nash and exhibited at the Academy in 1828 showing the castle with 'the Regatta Beating to Windward' (Indianapolis Museum of Art; B&J242) and 'the Regatta Starting from their Moorings' (Victoria and Albert Museum; B&J243). This sketch is the most developed of three made in anticipation of the first of these pictures. Yacht races at Cowes were still novel and exciting, having been held for the first time in 1826 even though their organiser, the Royal Yacht Club, had been founded as early as 1812. Turner's enthusiastic interest in the races is also evident from the drawings, and annotations of the names of boats and their owners and descriptions of their colours, in his *Windsor and Cowes* sketchbook used in 1827.

At East Cowes, Turner followed a practice he may already have used for his large Thames sketches (e.g. cat.nos.7 and 8) and returned to again for Italian subjects in 1828 (e.g. cat.nos.17 and 18); painting across long strips of canvas supplied and subsequently stored rolled. That summer Turner wrote to his father asking him to send down to the Isle of Wight one or if possible two pieces of unstretched canvas, either one of 6 by 4 feet, or a 'whole length'. He wanted the 'canvass only' and asked for it to be sent 'rolled up on a small roller'. In the event he received a 6 by 4 feet canvas, and it was on this, divided into two strips, that he painted the nine sketches of Cowes subjects (N01993–02001; B&J260–8) including this example and the following. Until rediscovered and divided at the National Gallery in 1905, these remained rolled on the two strips.

As so often with Turner's oil sketches, it has been suggested that the artist painted them on the spot. The viewpoint is generally from off-shore, some way out in Cowes Roads, so that the practical difficulties would have been considerable even if Turner were not managing a larger roll of canvas without a stretched support. However, he could have painted them from a bigger ship moored off-shore – perhaps the man-of-war whose decks and gun-ports are seen in the following sketch.

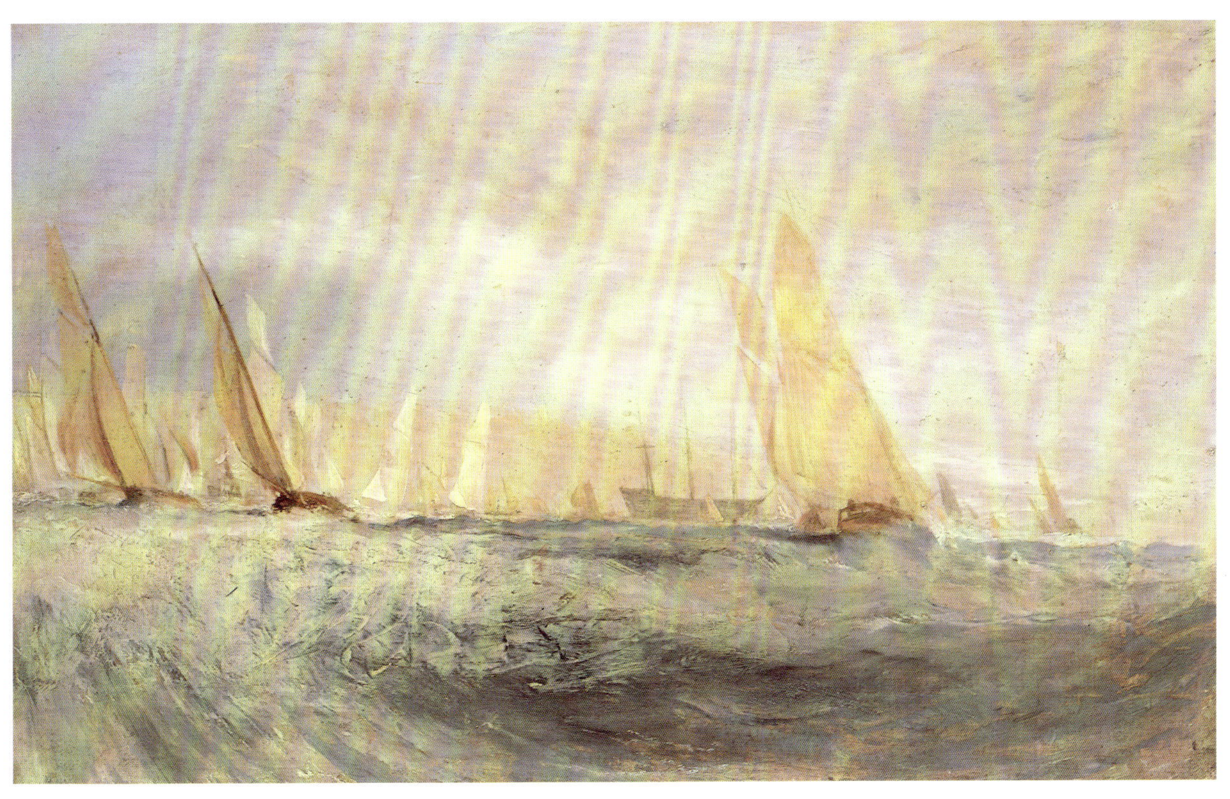

15 Between Decks 1827

Oil on canvas 305 × 485 ($12 \times 19\frac{1}{8}$)

N 01996

Turner may have painted some of his Cowes sketches from the vantage point of a ship such as the naval vessel whose lower deck is seen here. A naval guardship appears in the background of the three sketches for John Nash's picture of 'East Cowes Castle, the Regatta Beating to Windward' (see cat.no.14), and perhaps this is a scene on board. The ladies may be visitors to the ship, or possibly sailors' wives, for it had been navy practice up to about 1805 to accommodate them between the upper and lower decks while their husbands' ship was in port. This scene is marked by an immediacy and impromptu spirit that is rather rare in Turner's oil sketches, which, however spontaneous in execution, are usually conditioned by considerations of composition and design.

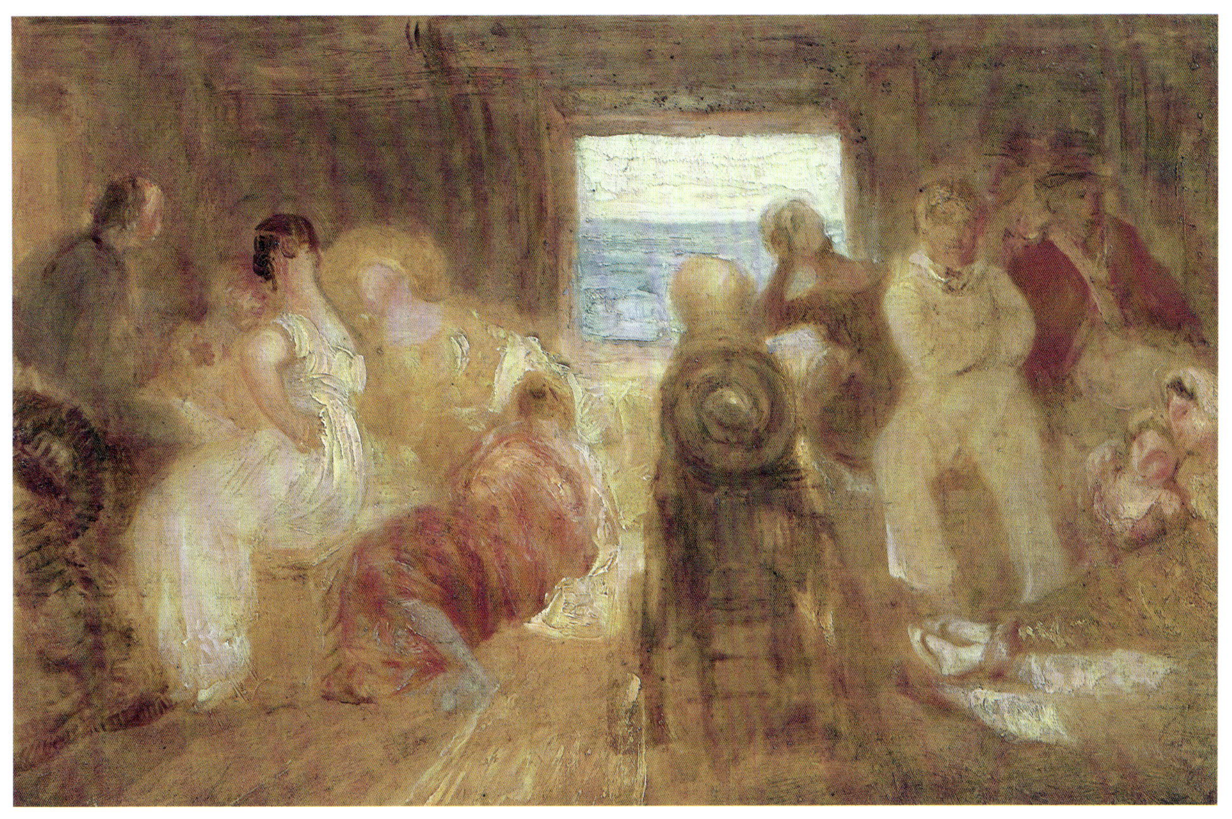

16   Southern Landscape with Aqueduct and Waterfall 1828

Oil on canvas 1500 × 2490 (59⅛ × 98⅛)
N 05506

Turner's first visit to Italy in 1819 did not apparently evoke any immediate response in oil. Instead, he concentrated on studying the country and its art, antiquities and people, and confided his observations to his sketchbooks. Back in Italy in 1828, however, he was active as a painter. In Rome he stayed with Charles Eastlake at 12 Piazza Mignanelli, and the following February Eastlake wrote that his fellow painter had exhibited three works and begun 'eight or ten pictures' while in the city. The exhibited works were 'View of Orvieto', 'Vision of Medea' and 'Regulus' (N 00511, 00513, 00515; B & J 292–4), all of which are on a characteristic coarse canvas, evidently of Italian manufacture, and share a similar type of stretcher and method of fixing the canvas to it by upholsterer's springs. These features are also to be found in some other quite large unfinished pictures which must be among the 'eight or ten' mentioned by Eastlake. Among these are three landscape studies which are too large, and generally too developed, to be regarded as oil sketches, but are more probably designs intended for finishing but never brought to completion. Of these, this subject is the only one which cannot definitely be said to have been painted in Rome, for although the canvas is of the Roman type, the original edges and stretcher have disappeared. However, the design, tonality and handling of the picture are entirely consistent with the Roman works, and like these, it bears evidence of having been rolled, perhaps for transport back to England by land whereas stretched canvases were sent home by sea.

The double perspective of river and roadway, divided by trees and a cascade, and the high tower at left, may connect the picture with another almost certainly painted, if not exhibited, in Rome; 'Palestrina – Composition', painted for Lord Egremont but not acquired by him, and exhibited at the Academy in 1830 (N 06283; B & J 295). Turner had wanted to paint Lord Egremont a companion to a work by Claude in his collection, and this canvas and the two similar large Italian landscapes could have been alternative composition studies for the project. The composition seems to be generally imaginary, a conflation of Italian scenic beauties, although the two-tiered aqueduct may have been inspired by the one between Nepi and Civita Castellana which Turner had seen and drawn on his way to Rome; the tower at left may also be that of the *rocca* at Nepi itself.

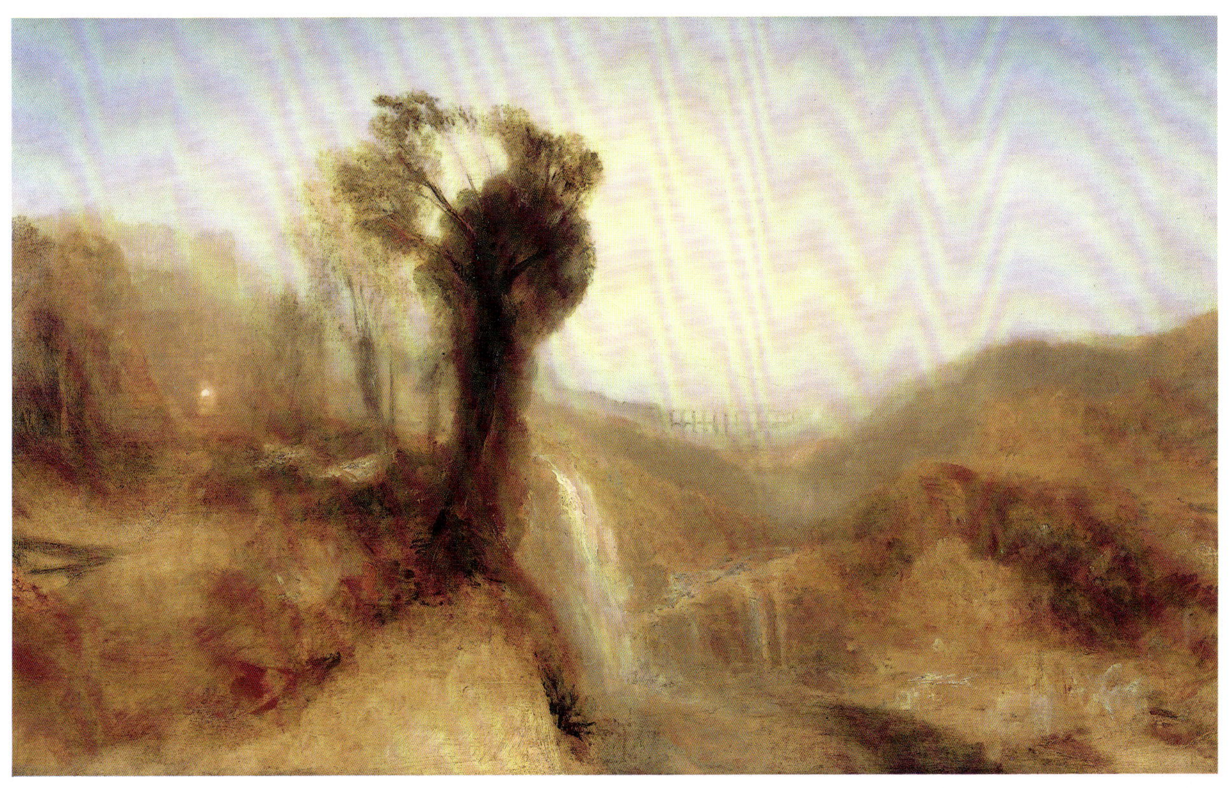

17   ?Ariccia: Sunset 1828

Oil on canvas 605 × 795 (23⅞ × 31¼)

N 02990

Besides large finished pictures, composition studies
and sketches, a group of sixteen smaller sketches is
generally associated with Turner's second visit to Italy
in 1828. Seven of these, including this subject, were
originally on one large piece of canvas as had been the
case with the Cowes sketches of 1827; they were kept
rolled, and were separated between 1913 and 1914. The
other nine are not recorded as having been rolled in this
way. All these sketches are essentially compositional
studies, distinctly pictorial in design and often evocative of the pastorals and seaports of Claude, rather
than studies from nature like the Cowes sketches or the
earlier Thames valley subjects appear to be. Their
simple masses and strong contrasts of light and shade,
and flat blocks of colour dabbed with impasto, are
quite distinctive, and show Turner working at a con-
ceptual level, devising a range of characteristic or ideal
images, and of tonal effects, by which to communicate
the spirit of Italy and the classical tradition. Whether
or not these sketches were intended as sample studies
to show to prospective clients – rather as Turner subsequently made sample versions of subjects in watercolour – they would have served him as a continuing
source of inspiration for finished pictures. Certainly
the main purpose of these sketches was not top-
ographical, and there is no sound evidence for the ten-
tative identification of this hill town as Ariccia near
Rome. There was no viaduct at Ariccia until 1854 and
the main features of the place, the square pile of the
Palazzo Chigi and the dome and towers of Bernini's
S. Maria dell'Assunzione, are not recognisable on the
skyline. If anything, the scenery in this sketch is closer
to that around Nepi (see also cat.no.16).

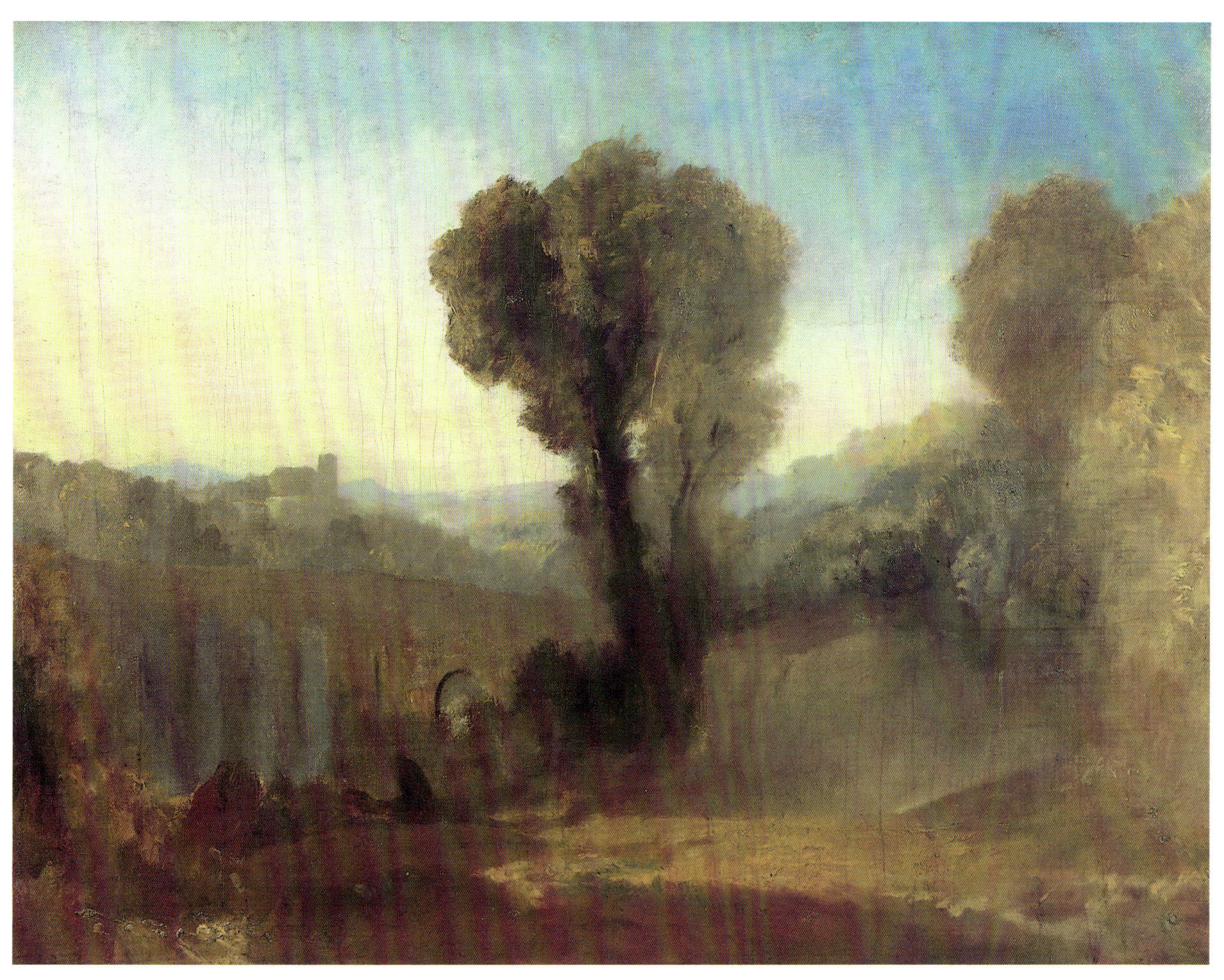

18   **Archway with Trees by the Sea** 1828

Oil on canvas

600×875 $(23\frac{5}{8} \times 34\frac{1}{4})$

N 03381

This sombre and atmospheric work is another of the group of Italian composition studies probably painted on one long roll of canvas in Rome in 1828. Only one of this series (N 02958; B & J 302) has been identified as a study for a finished picture, 'Ulysses Deriding Polyphemus' exhibited in the Academy in 1829 (National Gallery; B & J 330). However, this example seems more than coincidentally similar to the composition adopted later in 'The Parting of Hero and Leander' exhibited in 1837 (B & J 370). The banked terraces and arch at left, the tower overlooking the sea, the dark and turbulent waters of the Hellespont at night, and the pale, cold moonlight effect, are all anticipated here, and leaning over the parapet near the centre is a figure holding a torch such as appears in the finished picture. The tragic lovers Hero and Leander had been in Turner's mind for some years, and he may have been moved to consider them anew by William Etty's picture 'The Parting of Hero and Leander', exhibited at the Academy in 1827 (Tate Gallery; N 05614). Byron's swim across the Hellespont in 1810 may also have been an inspiration, together with his lines on Hero and Leander in the second canto of his poem *The Bride of Abydos* published in 1813. Turner had perhaps already come across the ancient poem on the lovers by the Greek grammarian, Musaeus, which he adapted himself to accompany his 1837 picture. A combination of ideas no doubt moved him to project their story on to a coastal subject that, like the sketch for 'Ulysses Deriding Polyphemus', was probably vaguely based on the tall cliffs and rocky arches he had seen around the Bay of Naples during his Italian tour of 1819. In working up a composition study like this, Turner depended on memory and imagination and not, as in some other oil sketches, on study from nature.

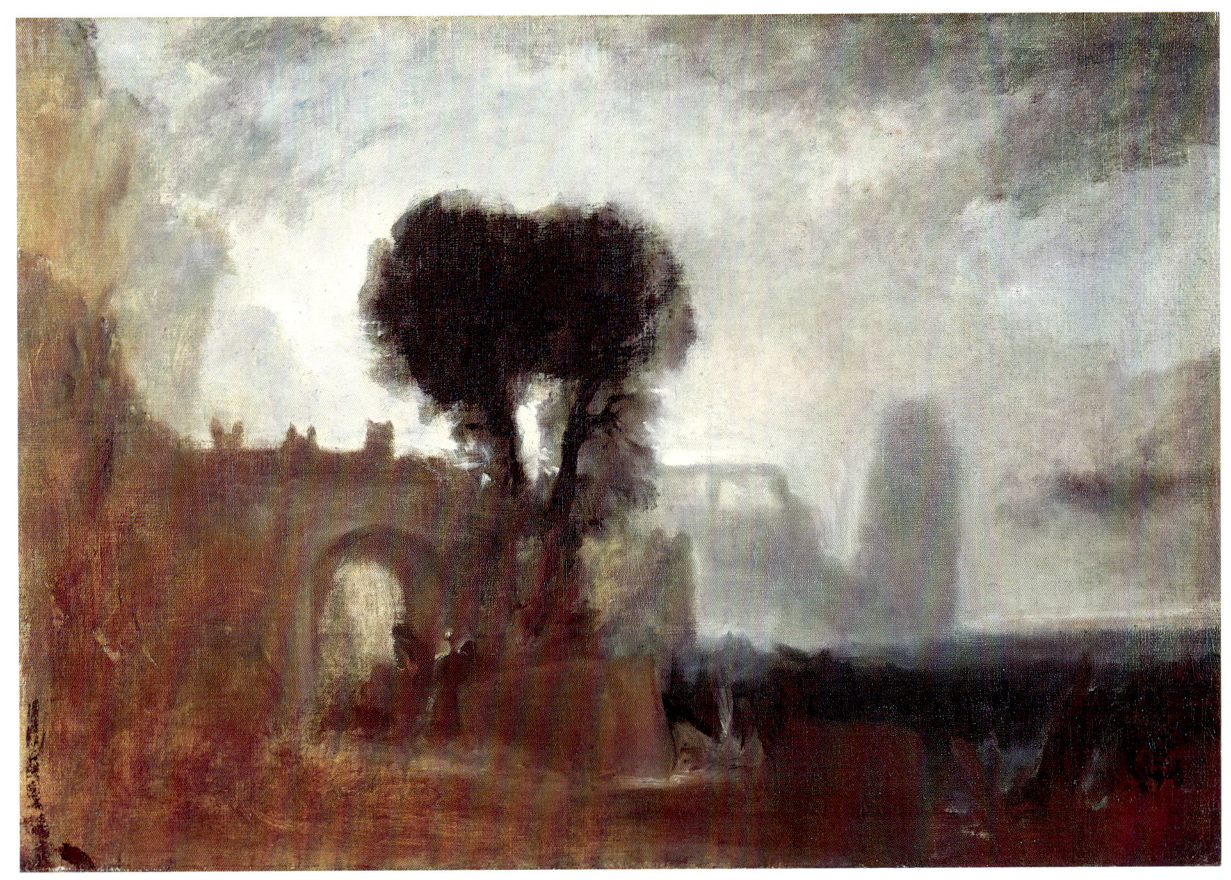

19   **Rocky Bay with Figures** *c.*1830

Oil on canvas 915 × 1245 (36 × 49)

N 01989

In subject this picture appears to be a development
from the composition studies probably made in Rome
in 1828 (see cat.nos.17, 18). Turner often used a canvas
3 by 4 feet for his exhibition and finished pictures, and
this is probably a work carried some considerable way
to completion rather than an independent sketch. The
sky is as fully finished and subtly modulated in its tone
and cloud effect as the skies in exhibited pictures of the
late 1820s and early 1830s, and the paint surface has
been worked over while still wet with brush handle,
palette knife or fingers to produce great variety of tone.
Turner was evidently moving towards a subject picture, for there is a figure standing in a rhetorical pose,
perhaps addressing a group of others on the shore at
left, and there are hints of long, low ships across the
water at right. These appear to be of ancient design,
and Turner may have had in mind an episode from the
story of Ulysses. The coastal scenery is clearly Mediterranean, and akin to that used in 'Ulysses Deriding Polyphemus' (see under cat.no.18).

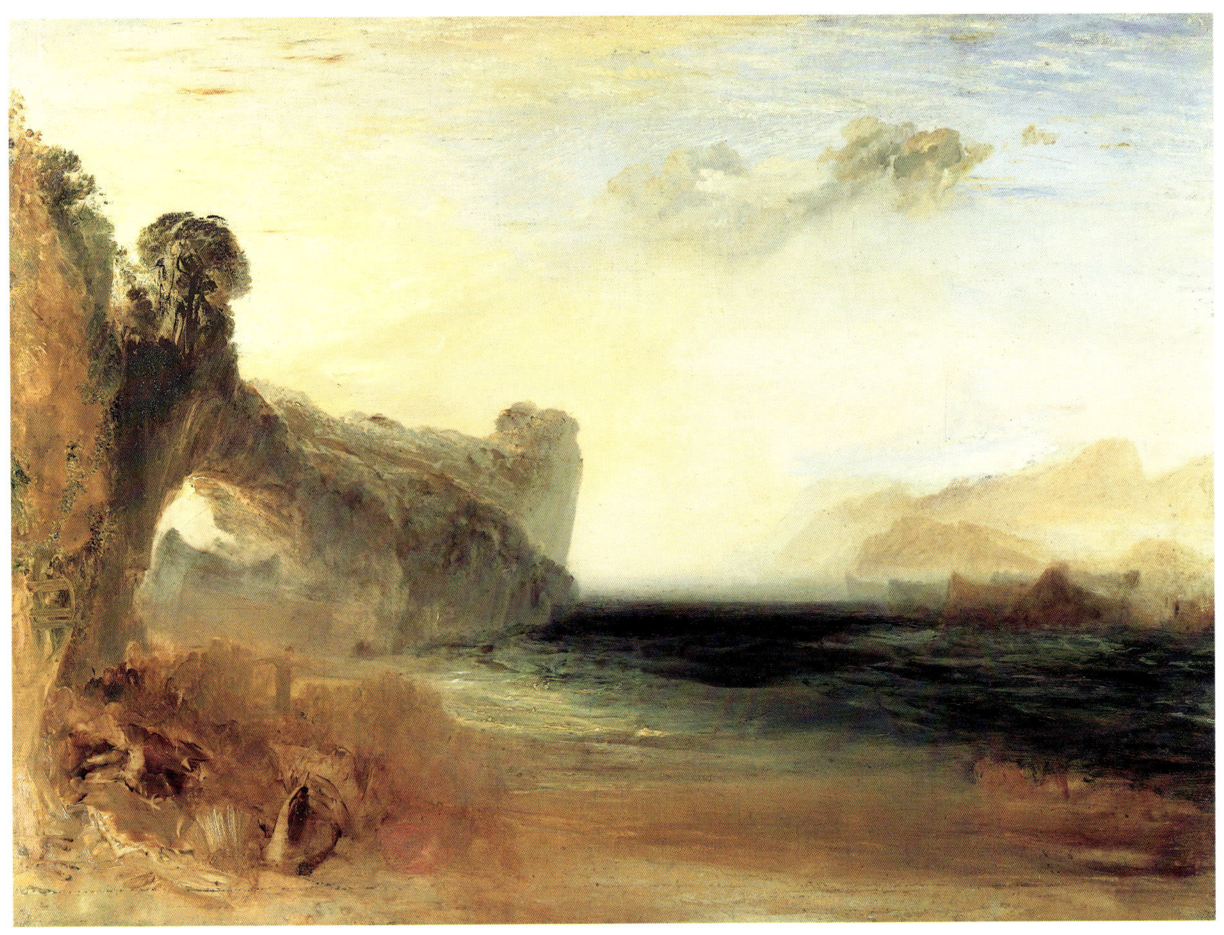

20 Van Tromp Returning after the Battle of the Dogger Bank Exh. 1833

Oil on canvas 905 × 1210 ($35\frac{5}{8} \times 47\frac{1}{2}$)

N 00537

Exhibited at the Royal Academy in 1833, this was the third of four pictures devoted to episodes in the career of 'Van' Tromp. These fit into a wider context of pictures concerned with Dutch history, and dependent on the tradition of Dutch marine painting. Turner had long been master of historic landscape; this picture shows him creating a type of 'historic marine'. Various historicising trends are to be found in Turner's finished pictures of the 1830s, and 'pure' history and art history are often combined. Besides continuing to drink at the fountain of Claude and the classical tradition, Turner had begun to explore the art of Antoine Watteau and to pay renewed attention to Rembrandt – both painters of the figure, but contrasted in style and technique, and both painters whose work had found modern followers in Turner's contemporaries Thomas Stothard and George Jones. The Dutch marine tradition represented another extreme when contrasted to Rembrandt, not least in the cool and silvery palette that Turner has so effectively adopted in this picture. Here too Turner's interest was sharpened by rivalry with contemporaries like Callcott and the young Clarkson Stanfield who had also formed much of their work on Dutch marine painting. Turner's involvement with it, as with other historical or traditional styles, was all the keener for this lively spirit of competition.

It was characteristic of Turner to add a gloss of 'historical' episode or anecdote to a work in an historical style; the same year he had alluded to one of his stylistic sources, the Dutch seventeenth century painter Jan van Goyen, in another Academy exhibit, 'Van Goyen, Looking Out for a Subject' (Frick Collection, New York; B & J 350), and in his 'Van' Tromp pictures he turned to scenes from the life of a Dutch admiral of the same period. The first of these, 'Admiral Van Tromp's Barge at the Entrance to the Texel, 1645' (Sir John Soane's Museum, London; B & J 339) was exhibited in 1831; the second, 'Van Tromp's Shallop, at the Entrance to the Scheldt' (Wadsworth Atheneum, Hartford, Connecticut; B & J 344), was shown in 1832; the present picture appeared the next year; and in 1844 Turner completed the series with 'Van Tromp, Going About to Please his Masters' (Royal Holloway College; B & J 410). The last was exhibited with a reference to a lost or spurious art-historical source, *Lives of the Dutch Painters*, and Turner's characteristically cavalier attitude to historical fact – as opposed to atmosphere – had been in evidence throughout this series of pictures. There was no Admiral 'Van' Tromp, and Turner was evidently referring to Maarten Harpertzoon Tromp (1597–1653), or to his son Cornelis (1629–1691) – or had perhaps confused or combined the two. However, neither could have fought at the Battle of the Dogger Bank, which took place in 1781.

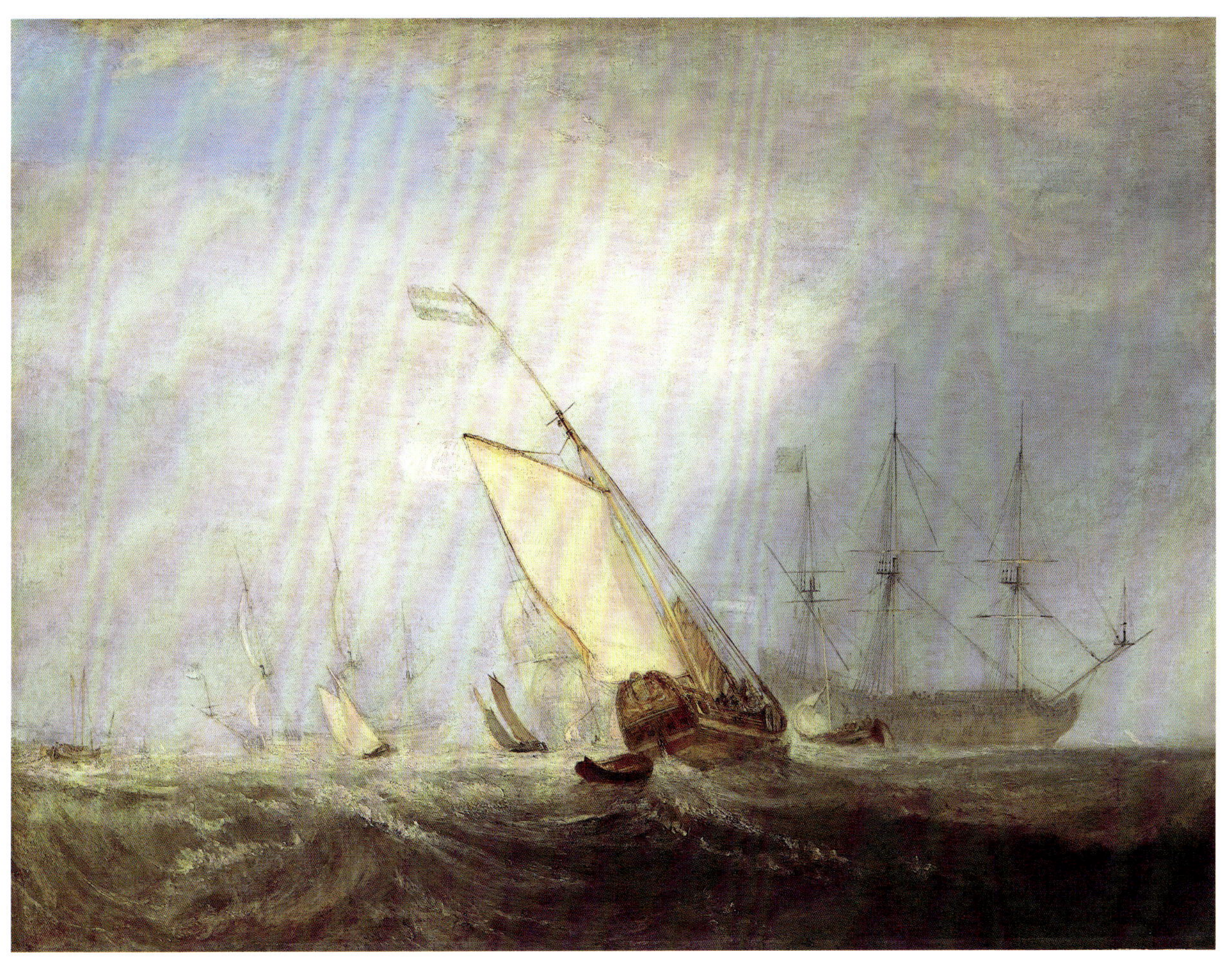

21   **Dinner in a Great Room, with Figures in Costume** *c*.1830–5

Oil on canvas 910 × 1220 (35¾ × 48)

N 05502

This painting is on a canvas of Turner's standard 3 by 4 feet format, and in parts is quite developed in execution. But although evidently more than an oil sketch, it was never exhibited by Turner and its subject and status must remain uncertain. It belongs to a group of paintings of figures in interiors, and sometimes in historical costume, that have generally been associated with Turner's visits to Lord Egremont at Petworth in the 1830s, and in some cases with his stay with John Nash at East Cowes Castle in 1827 (see cat.no.14). The convivial life in both houses, with parties, dinners and gatherings by lamp and firelight – captured most vividly in a famous series of drawings in bodycolour on blue paper made at Petworth (TB CCXLIV) – seems to have merged in Turner's mind with his interest in artists associated with subjects of human drama and narrative like Watteau, and of dramatically contrasted lighting effects like Rembrandt. Among contemporary painters, Turner had been greatly impresssed by Richard Parkes Bonington, whose small pictures of historical figures in interiors had appeared in the Academy in the 1820s and, after the painter's death, in sales in 1829 and 1834. Moreover, a frequent guest at Petworth was the American painter Charles Robert Leslie, who had established himself as a painter of historical narrative in a more popular or sentimental vein. Leslie was among a number of artists who contributed to another contemporary trend of which Turner was well aware, the *Keepsake* annuals with their small engraved illustrations of subjects from romantic literature.

All these factors played a part in developing Turner's interest in painting figures in interiors, although he had only recently remarked, 'Figures are not my style'. Here the prevailing influence is evidently Rembrandt. The arched room and dramatic shafts of light against which figures are seen in silhouette, are clearly inspired by that master. In some respects the grouping of the figures and the architectural setting recall Turner's still more Rembrandt-like 'Pilate Washing his Hands' exhibited in 1830 (N 00510; B & J 332), but the figures here seem to be wearing more specifically seventeenth century costume and to be engaged in largely social activities around a table. On the other hand, a sombre mood prevails throughout, and another picture of the same size and very similar in handling, tone, and the scale and dress of the figures, appears to be set in a vault or dungeon ('Figures in a Building'; N 05496; B & J 446). The subjects of these canvases are evidently not resolved; they are most probably investigations of the compositional and atmospheric possibilities of a type of historical narrative that was newly fashionable and with which Turner was not yet wholly at ease.

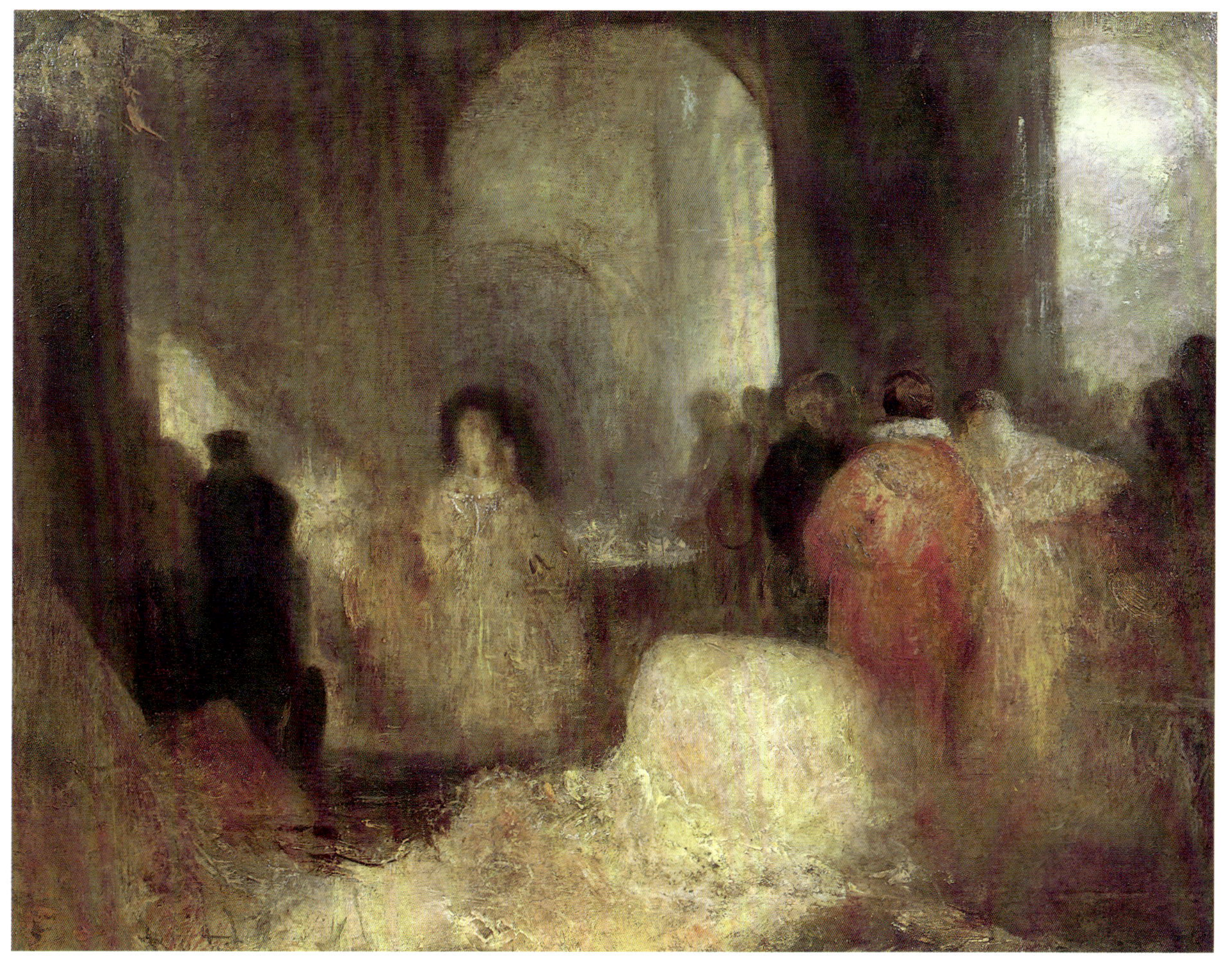

22   The Arch of Constantine, Rome *c.1835*

Oil on canvas 910 × 1220 (36 × 48)

N 02066

This is one of two Italian landscapes on Turner's standard 3 by 4 feet canvases, carried almost to the point of completion to exhibition standard but then apparently abandoned. The other is a composition of 'Tivoli: Tobias and the Angel' (N 02067; B & J 437). The pictures were clearly designed as a pair as they are complementary in composition and in their brilliant colouring, which is probably nearer to the original than is the case in the majority of oils. The exact relationship of the subject matter is not certain as there is no obvious counterpart here for the religious content of the 'Tivoli'; however, the ghostly figure to right of centre has sometimes been interpreted as a protagonist in a Resurrection scene. Turner's continuing interest in the classical tradition and the ideal symmetry of Claude's landscapes is manifest in both pictures, although the handling and colouring are no longer Claudean. The pictures were presumably worked up from memory and are generally thought to have been painted in the mid 1830s on comparison with the dense and bold handling of the oils of that period usually associated with Turner's visits to Petworth (see cat.no.21).

Turner had made a number of careful drawings of the Arch of Constantine, one of the main features of the Roman Forum. Here, however, he has so far discounted its surface details, hardly defining the freestanding statues on its attic storey, and its medallion reliefs. Instead it appears as a generalised mass, catching the evening light.

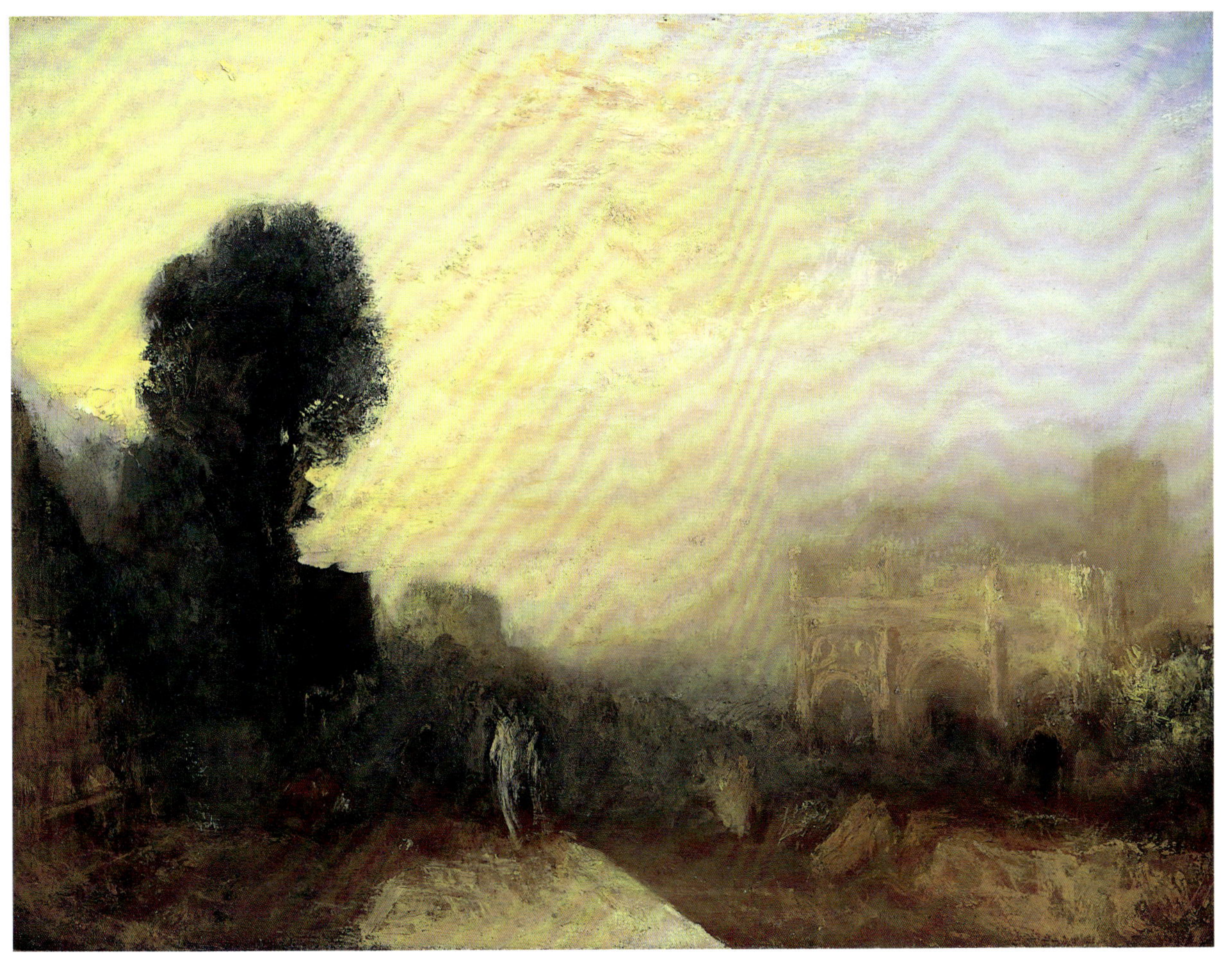

23   **Waves Breaking on a Lee Shore** *c.*1835

Oil on canvas 600 × 950 ($23\frac{1}{2}$ × $37\frac{1}{2}$)

N 02882

In his later years Turner became increasingly preoccupied with painting the sea, not only as the setting for
finished marine compositions, but in its own right as a
natural element moved by wind or tide. Waves,
breakers or, sometimes, calm expanses of water were
studied or sketched in a long series of oils and watercolours. Turner was encouraged in these – which were
more often undertaken for his own interest than with
any finished works in mind – by his regular visits to
Margate during the 1830s and 1840s. There he stayed
with his landlady and mistress Mrs Booth, in a house
overlooking the harbour, and the changing moods of
sea and sky were a constant source of fascination and
delight. A large number of oil studies of stormy seas
date from the mid 1830s to about 1845. The chrono-
logy is by no means certain, but the bold handling and
bright colouring of this example probably indicates a
date near the beginning of this period. A very similar
study of waves, on the same unusual wide landscape
format, is evidently its companion (N 02881; B & J 457).

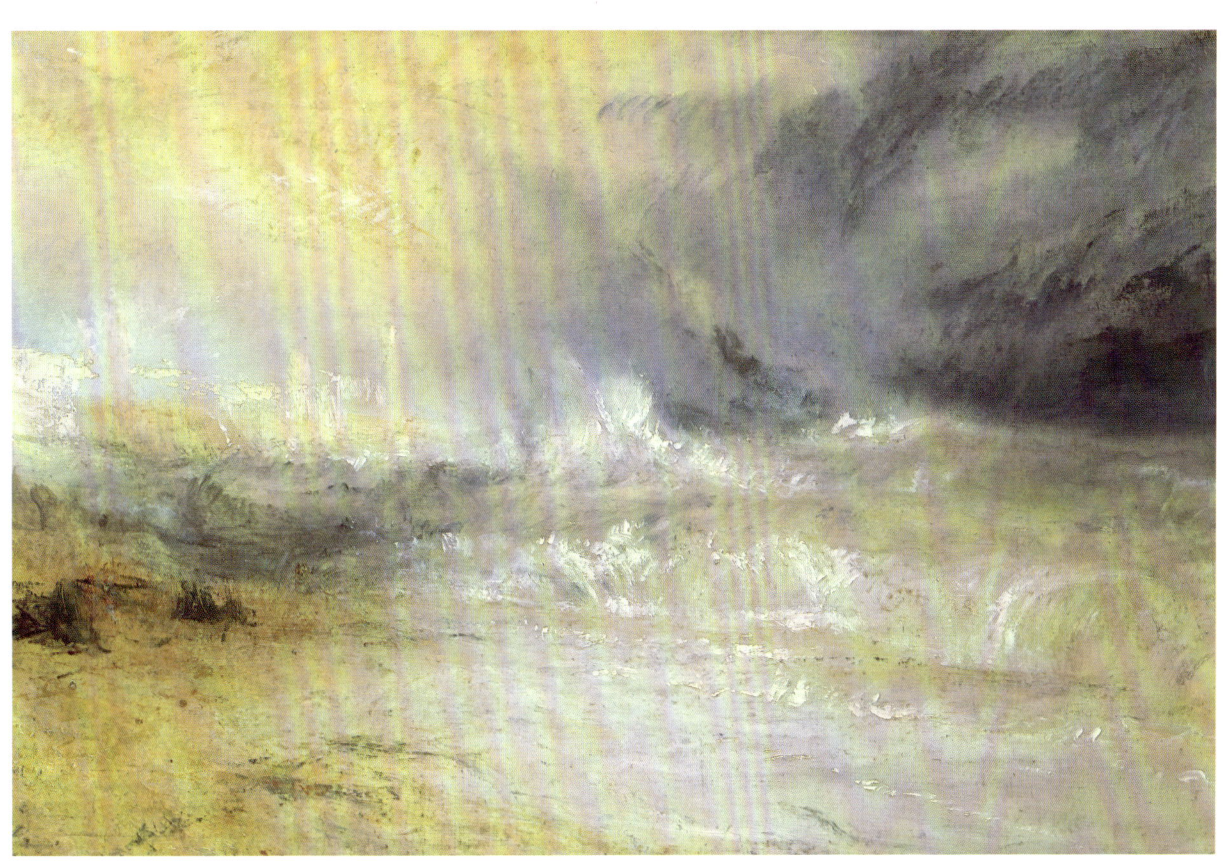

24 **Rough Sea** *c.*1840–5

Oil on canvas 915 × 1220 (36 × 48)

N 05479

Among Turner's late sea paintings is a group on his standard 3 by 4 feet canvases, but which appear by no means finished and are in fact among the boldest and most 'impressionistic' of all his works in oil. Of these none has more powerful a sense of immediacy and dramatic engagement in its subject than this picture. In a few crisp, striated brushstrokes and vigorous bursts of impasto Turner marvellously conjures waves beating against a pier or breakwater, and conveys the foggy dampness and cold, wintery light that permeates the scene. There has been considerable loss of white and red paint in the foreground; had these passages survived the picture might have presented a slightly more finished appearance, but although by the mid 1840s Turner had broken down many conventional distinctions between 'finished' and 'unfinished', the canvas lacked the specific subject and reference he considered essential in exhibited work.

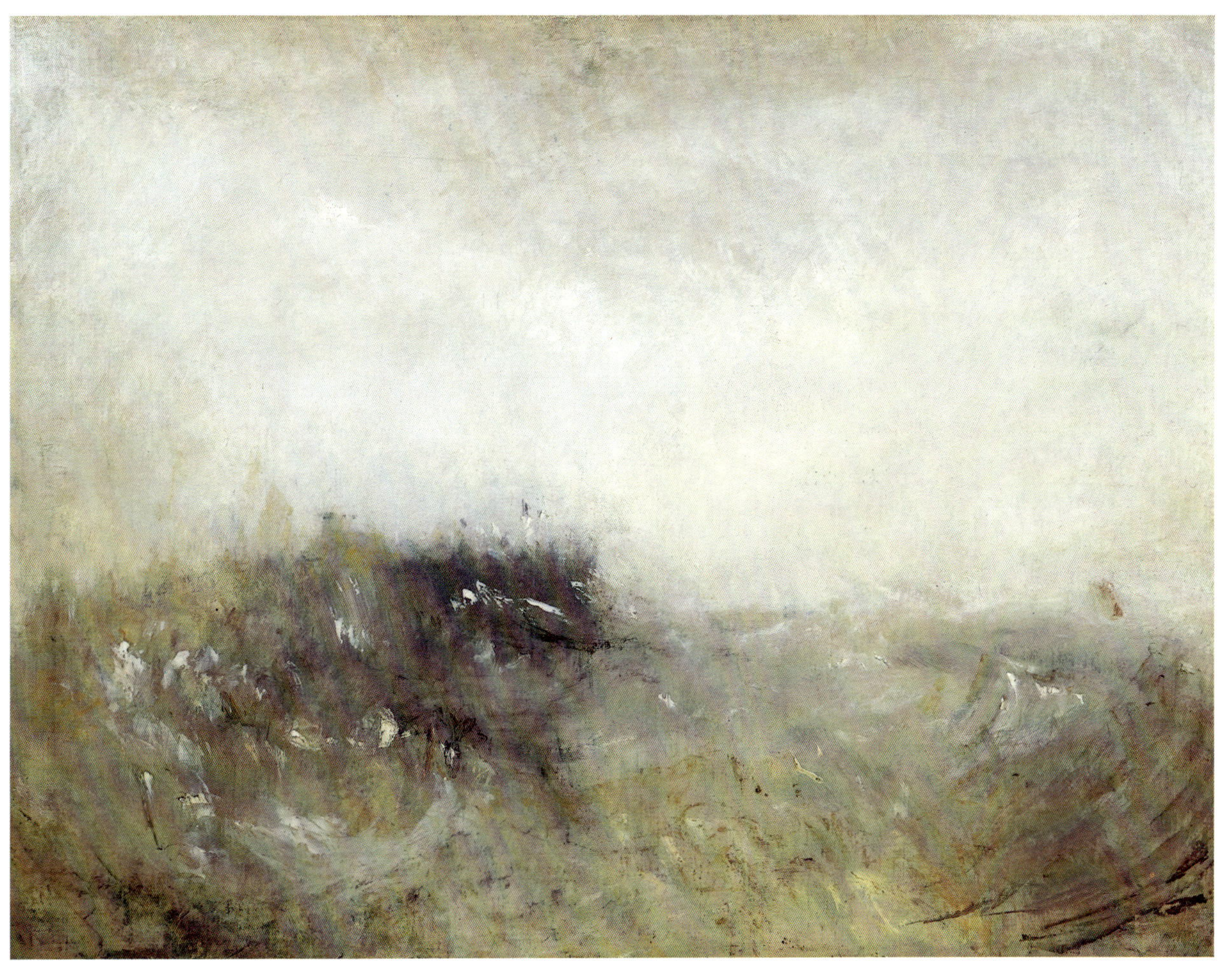

25   **Figures on a Beach** *c.*1840–5

Oil on millboard 260 × 300 (10$\frac{3}{16}$ × 11$\frac{3}{4}$)

D 36690

Besides his sea sketches on canvas and in watercolour in his sketchbooks, Turner also made, probably in the early to mid 1840s, a series of fourteen perfunctory, but marvellously evocative oil sketches of beach and coast scenes on millboard. He used three basic sizes of millboard panel, of which this example is one of the smallest. The sketches vary somewhat in finish and effect, being sometimes little more than studies of tonal relationships, laid in with almost blank fields of colour, and on other occasions containing the merest hints of figures or sails. Here, a few dabs of darker colour suggest figures hauling in a boat or a fishing net at the water's edge. None of these sketches can have any more than a coincidental connection with Turner's larger or more developed oil paintings of the 1840s; they do however represent another, and technically distinctive aspect of the interest in coastal scenery and effects that came to the fore in the first half of that decade. The habitual viewpoint looking out to sea, and the motifs of glistening sands, breaking waves, solitary distant ships or beachcombing figures that occur in these oil sketches are matched in large numbers of watercolour impressions in his sketchbooks, above all those used in 1845 during spring and autumn visits to the Kent coast, and across the Channel to Boulogne, Dieppe and Picardy. The closest parallels are to be found in the so-called *Channel* sketchbook probably used that year and once owned by Turner's Margate friend, Mrs Booth (Yale Center for British Art, U.S.A.).

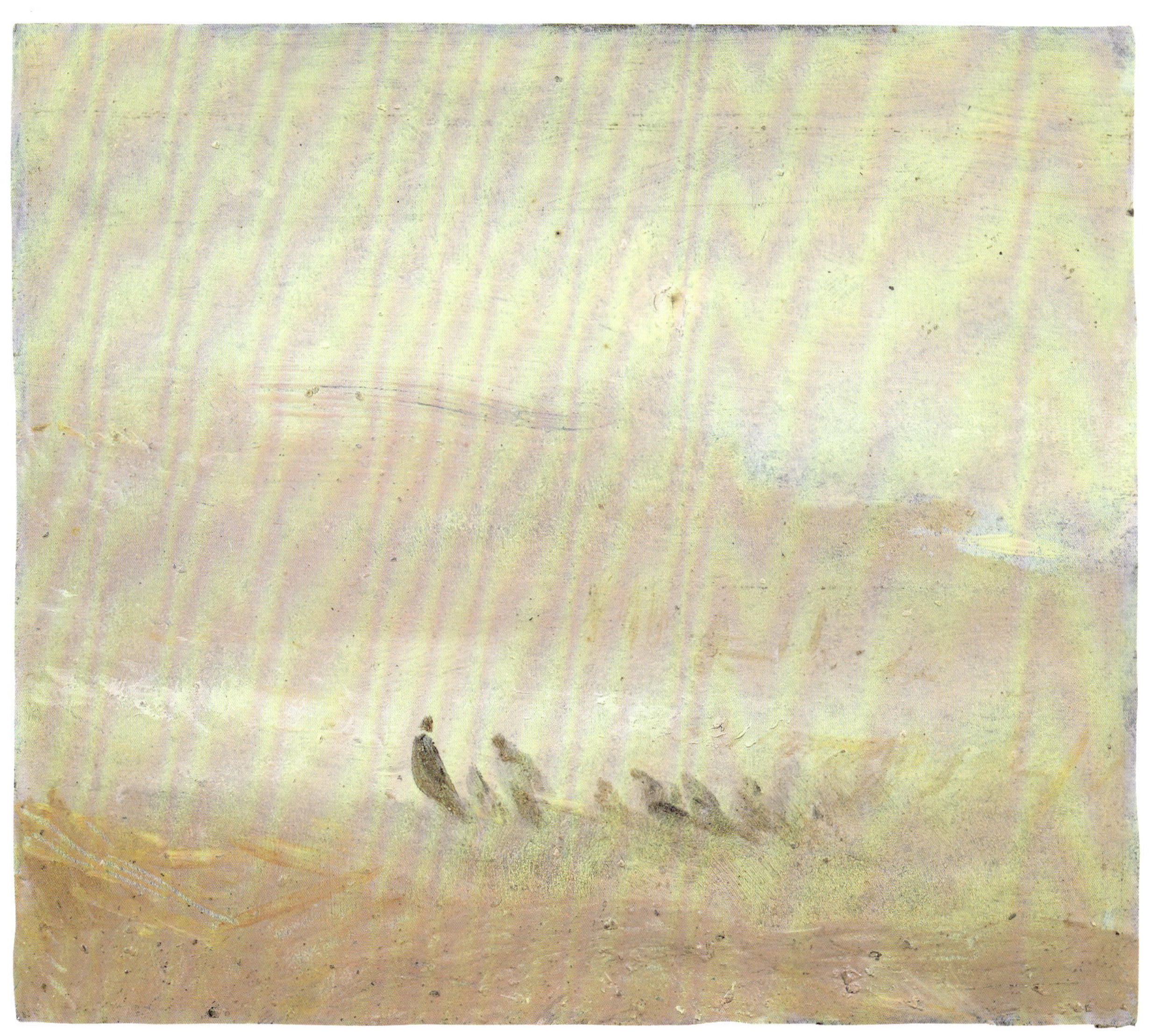

26 Sunrise, a Boat between Headlands

c.1840–5

Oil on canvas 915 × 1220 (36 × 48)

N 02002

As a young man, out to impress and to exploit the medium of his choice to its fullest possible effect, Turner had striven to carry watercolour to the density, richness of colour and sheer scale usually associated with oil painting. In his later years, by contrast, his use of oil itself became increasingly modified by the example of his mature handling of watercolour. Just as his watercolour manner had become infinitely more sensitive and finely distilled, combining breadth and luminosity with passages of fine brushwork or strokes of the pen to suggest texture or detail, so his handling of oil, at least in pictures that remained unfinished, can be seen to have taken over many of the same characteristics. This is particularly evident in this painting, which is itself perhaps a development from some of Turner's watercolours of Swiss lakes made in the 1840s; the mountains and the prominent headland to the right, probably surmounted by a tower or castle, could have been selected from a number of drawings, and seem to have been combined, as so often in Turner's last paintings, to create a theatre of light. Rather than a sketch, this may be a work left unfinished, on Turner's standard 3 by 4 feet canvas. It was in just this state that Turner took his late pictures to the Royal Academy and the British Institution before completing them on Varnishing Days. The engraver John Burnet describes such pictures, in their preliminary stage, as 'divided into large masses of blue, where the water or sky was to come, and the other portions laid out in broad orange yellow, falling into delicate brown where the trees and landscapes were to be placed'.

27 Sunrise, a Castle on a Bay: 'Solitude'

c.1840–5

Oil on canvas 910 × 1220 (35¾ × 48)

N 01985

In about the mid 1840s Turner, in retrospective mood, made a series of nine paintings based on plates originally published in his compendium of landscape styles, the *Liber Studiorum*. The *Liber* had been intended to demonstrate the range of landscape types from the ideal to the rustic or naturalistic. Now, Turner turned particularly to plates he had classified as 'Pastoral', or 'Elevated', 'Epic' or 'Elegant Pastoral', and worked up a series of variants in oil that, in contrast to the turbulent seascapes, storms or apocalyptic themes that dominated much of his later painting, reasserted the value of idyllic, serene and light-filled landscape in the tradition of Claude. This was itself perhaps sufficient motive; on the other hand Turner was showing renewed interest in the *Liber* itself, and in May and June 1845 had fifteen new sets of the plates reprinted. It is also possible that Turner may by now have been at a loss for new subjects; but on the other hand again, the *Liber* variants might have been substantially altered in mood and content had Turner taken them any further. This possibility must certainly be borne in mind since these canvases are generally brought to exactly the state to which Turner took pictures intended for exhibition before completing them on Varnishing Days, although it has also been suggested that he painted them precisely to see whether there was a market for 'sketchy' pictures. This example, with its beautiful pattern of trees reverberating against light, is based on the plate 'Solitude', published 12 May 1814 in the 'EP' or higher Pastoral category of the *Liber*; Turner has here omitted the figure of the Magdalen, who in the print reclines in meditation beneath the trees to the left.

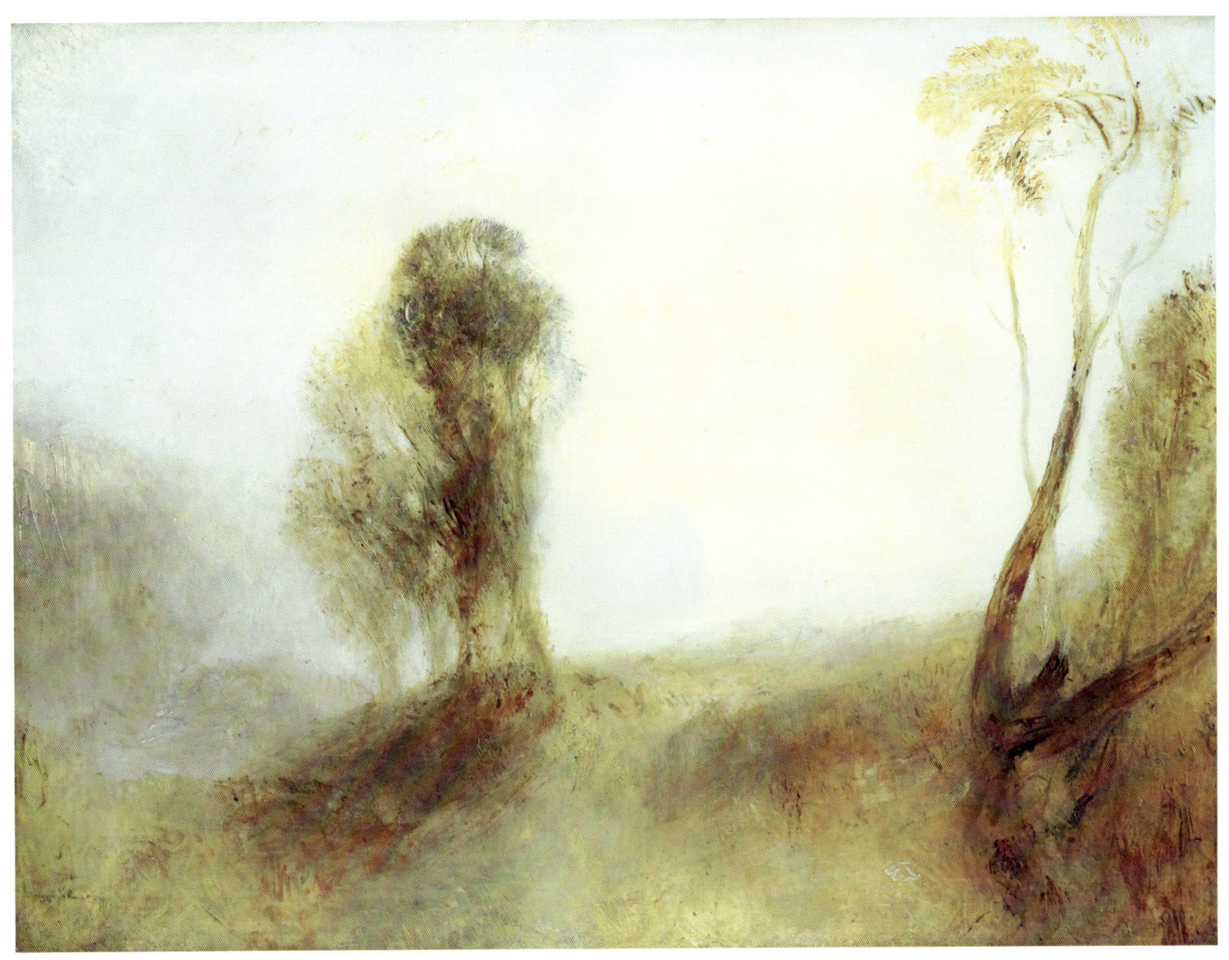

28   Venetian Scene *c.*1840–5

Oil on canvas 795 × 790 (31¼ × 31)

N 05482

This picture, evidently another unfinished work which could have been resolved further or considerably altered on a Varnishing Day, is on a square format Turner used a number of times in the 1840s, generally for exhibited pairs of pictures on complementary themes. The large field of sky is worked up with the palette knife and in curved sweeps of the brush that anticipate the vortex effects found in some of Turner's late pictures, but it is likely that he would have added much more colour and detail had he decided to take the picture to exhibition. As it is, even the subject remains very unclear. It has usually been considered a Venetian scene and related to a group of late oils of vaguely festive or processional subjects connected with the city, but Venetian features are far from explicit, and nor can one be sure that the foreground contains a procession of boats – the usual justification for the Venetian connection. It seems equally likely that Turner was working towards a group of figures, led by one in a red cloak, standing on a shore as if on the point of departure; this might suggest a classical subject. A rather Claudean river landscape with a bridge (N 05475; B & J 532) has sometimes been considered as a companion to this picture. However, there seems nothing in common in the subject matter, as far as it goes; and a more telling objection to the connection may be the fact that the horizon lines in the two pictures are quite different.

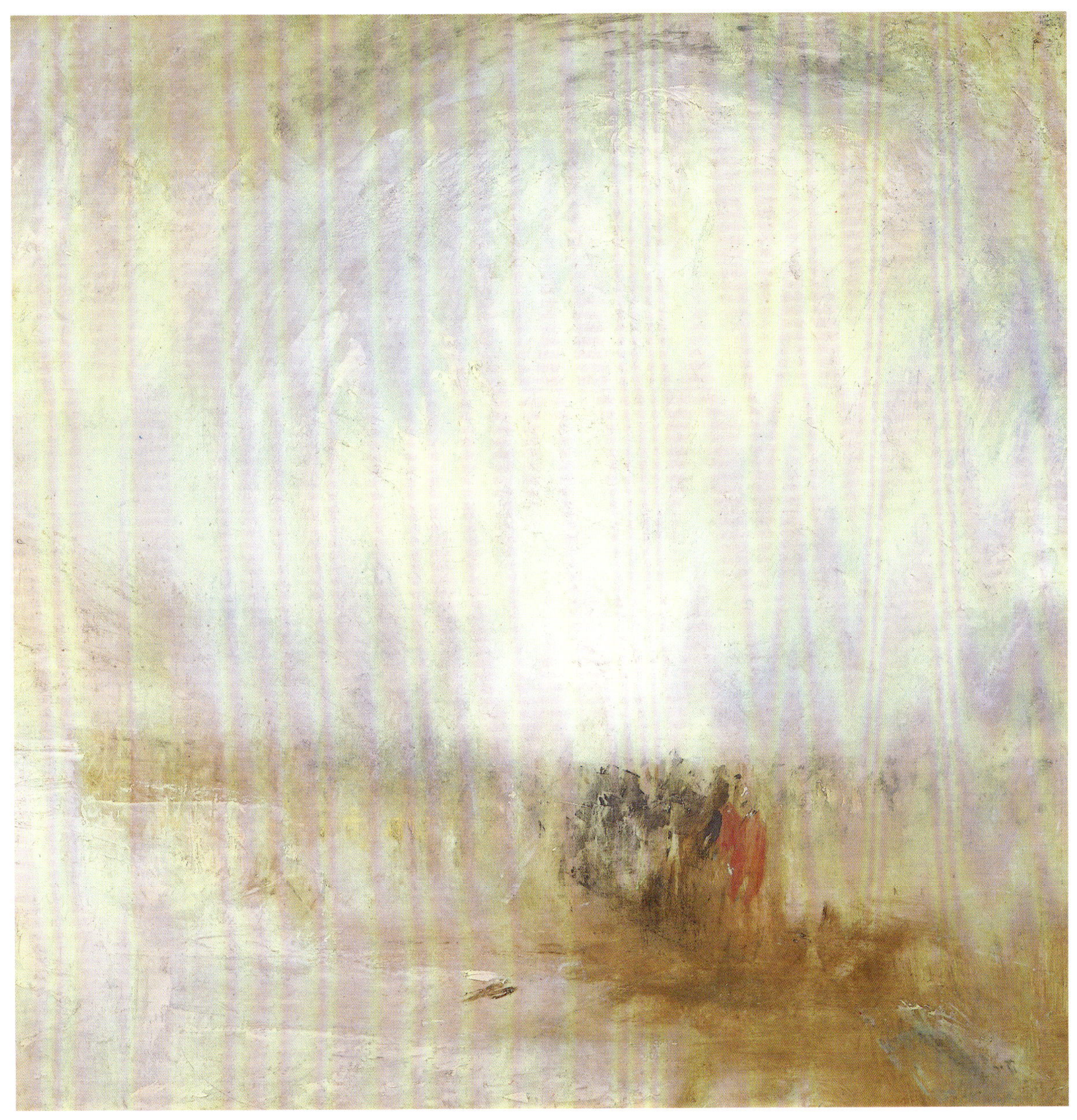

29 The Departure of the Fleet Exh. 1850

Oil on canvas 895 × 1205 (35⅜ × 47⅜)

N 00554

One of four pictures on the theme of Aeneas's stay at Carthage, tempted by his love for Dido to resist the destiny that summoned him to Italy; these were Turner's last exhibits at the Royal Academy in 1850. They were accompanied by lines from his manuscript poem *Fallacies of Hope*. In this case the quotation was:

The orient moon shone on the departing fleet,
Nemesis invoked, the priest held the poisoned cup.

Dido and her retinue, on the left, watch the fleet leave harbour. Turner had long been preoccupied with Carthaginian subjects, and these final pictures were the last of a long series of meditations on stylistic themes drawn from the seaports of Claude; the structure of these classic compositions can clearly be discerned here although it is overlaid with a rich, if very diffuse, web of detail and expressed in far more brilliant and jewel-like colour. Reviewers, whether favourable or not, recognised that Turner's approach was now fanciful, capricious and uniquely personal; but it is interesting that in these last paintings he should return to the old master who had perhaps most consistently inspired him.

The intricate detail and surface colour seen here was, by the 1840s, usually contributed on the Varnishing Days, working over canvases on which the essentials of form and tone had been broadly laid in. However, by 1850 Turner's health would not have permitted virtuoso displays in public at the Academy, and the elaboration of the Dido and Aeneas pictures may well have been done in Turner's last home in Cheyne Walk. The engraver and watercolourist J.W. Archer recalls at least three of them 'set in a row and he went from one to the other, first painting upon one, touching on the next, and so on, in rotation'.

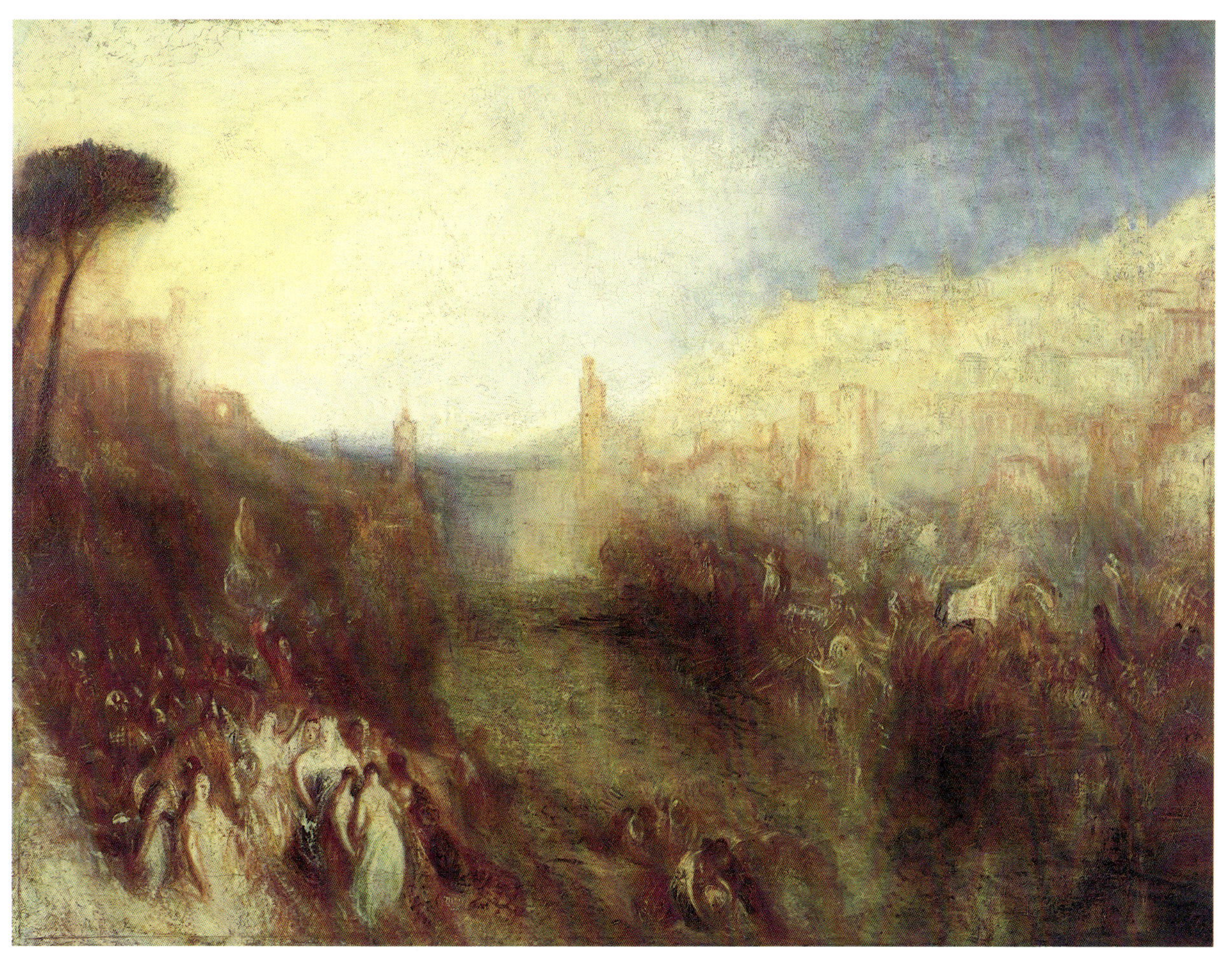